Microsoft® Access 2010:
Level 3 of 3

PAMELA R. TOLIVER
Soft-Spec, LLC

LABYRINTH
LEARNING™

El Sobrante, CA

Microsoft Access 2010: Level 3
by Pamela R. Toliver

Copyright © 2011 by Labyrinth Learning

Labyrinth Learning
P.O. Box 20818
El Sobrante, California 24820
800.522.9746
On the web at lablearning.com

President:
Brian Favro

Product Development Manager:
Jason Favro

Managing Editor:
Laura A. Lionello

Production Manager:
Rad Proctor

eLearning Production Manager:
Arl S. Nadel

Editorial/Production Team:
Donna Bacidore, Pamela Beveridge,
Belinda Breyer, Everett Cowan, Alec Fehl,
Alona Harris, Sandy Jones, PMG Media

Indexing: Joanne Sprott

Interior Design:
Mark Ong, Side-by-Side Studios

Cover Design:
Words At Work

ITEM: 1-59136-337-3
ISBN-13: 978-1-59136-337-8

Manufactured in the United States of America.

10 9 8 7 6 5 4 3 2 1

Table of Contents

Quick Reference Tables

Preface

Microsoft® Access 2010: Level 3 provides thorough training of Access 2010 advanced skills. This course is supported with comprehensive instructor resources and our eLab assessment and learning management tool. And, our new work-readiness exercises ensure students have the critical thinking skills necessary to succeed in today's world.

Visual Conventions

This book uses many visual and typographic cues to guide students through the lessons. This page provides examples and describes the function of each cue.

Type this text	Anything you should type at the keyboard is printed in this typeface.
	Tips, Notes, and Warnings are used throughout the text to draw attention to certain topics.
Command→ Command→ Command, etc.	This convention indicates how to give a command from the Ribbon. The commands are written: Ribbon Tab→Command Group→Command→ Subcommand.
FROM THE KEYBOARD Ctrl+S to save	These margin notes indicate shortcut keys for executing a task described in the text.

Exercise Progression

The exercises in this book build in complexity as students work through a lesson toward mastery of the skills taught.

- **Develop Your Skills** exercises are introduced immediately after concept discussions. They provide detailed, step-by-step tutorials.
- **Reinforce Your Skills** exercises provide additional hands-on practice with moderate assistance.
- **Apply Your Skills** exercises test students' skills by describing the correct results without providing specific instructions on how to achieve them.
- **Critical Thinking and Work-Readiness Skills** exercises are the most challenging. They provide generic instructions, allowing students to use their skills and creativity to achieve the results they envision.

A Note About Lesson and Page Numbering

You will notice that this book does not begin with Lesson 1 on page 1. This is not an error! The lessons in this book are part of a larger text. We have repackaged the large book into smaller books – while retaining the original lesson and page numbering – to accommodate classes of varying lengths and course hours.

All content in this book is presented in the proper, intended order.

Setting Up Complex Forms

LESSON OUTLINE

LEARNING OBJECTIVES

After studying this lesson, you will be able to:

- Create a main form containing a subform
- Edit a data source
- Format a form and add a logo
- Add a calculated field to a form
- Add the current date to the form
- Set form properties to disable, lock, add ScreenTips, hide form elements, and create pop-up forms

Forms provide a valuable input device for entering data into database tables, especially when those who enter the data are unfamiliar with the complex nature of database structures. In this lesson, you will learn some of the techniques database developers use to create input forms containing subforms that are both functional and aesthetically friendly to use. You will also review and explore many features available in Access to format forms, create calculated fields, replace data sources, disable and add tips to form controls, and set control properties to protect and limit data entry.

Formatting Functional Forms

Welcome to iJams, an online music distribution company where musicians send in originally recorded material on CDs or as MP3 files for distribution. iJams duplicates CDs as orders come in and makes MP3s available for immediate purchase and download. Musicians can send in digital artwork, and iJams will print full-color CD inserts and other support materials. Additionally, iJams sells promotional items such as T-shirts and mouse pads for artists. iJams has recently added music videos to its repertoire and expanded its inventory to include equipment on which to view or listen to these files.

Sales have increased over the past months, and the company has hired a new sales manager, Andrea Schuster. Andrea will work with Jin Chen, marketing analyst, and Brett Schneider, who is responsible for fulfillment, to develop and maintain a database for tracking inventory, customers, sales, and orders. Tables to hold data have been added to the iJams database, and sample data includes more than one hundred Houston, Texas customers, more than fifty inventory items, fifty sales representatives, and thirty-five orders.

Relationships have been established among the database tables. Now Andrea is designing forms to assist sales representatives with data entry. In this lesson, you will create forms that contain subforms so that sales representatives can track orders by customer and also create orders. The database relationships will aid in setting up these forms.

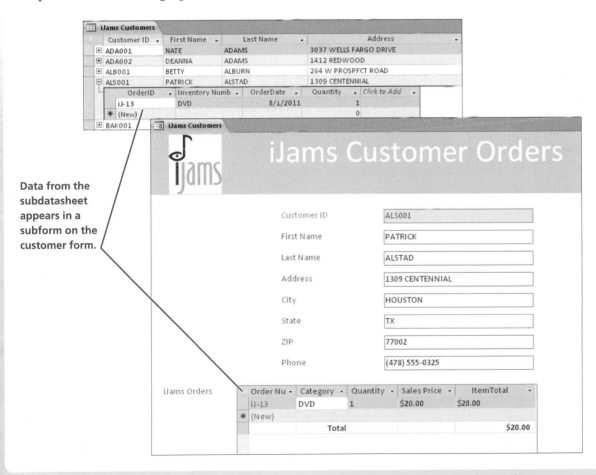

Data from the subdatasheet appears in a subform on the customer form.

9.1 Identifying Complex Form Features

Video Lesson labyrinthelab.com/videos

Getting data into a database so that you can obtain meaningful reports is important to the success of any database. Forms often serve as the interface between the user and the database and are the primary input object for entering, editing, and deleting records in Access databases. Tables and queries provide the underlying structure for creating most forms. Although many forms are designed to enter data into a single table, when you create forms that data entry personnel use to perform actions such as process customer orders, calculate payroll, and locate data, fields from multiple tables will normally appear on the form.

By now, you most likely have customized forms to place specific fields from a table or query where you want them on the form. You may have also arranged field controls and set the tab order on the form to streamline data entry, added pictures, dates, and titles to form headers and footers. Access contains additional features for formatting database forms that allow you to:

- Place a *subform* on a form to display a subset of data within a main form so that you can enter complete data for multiple tables from one form.
- Create tips to assist in data entry.
- Create calculated fields on forms that are similar to those you may have added to queries.
- Create pop-up forms that display when called upon to provide supplemental information.
- Disable form fields so that no one can edit the data.
- Hide screen elements.

9.2 Creating a Main Form Containing a Subform

As you have progressed through your study of Access, you have most likely used both Design View and wizards to create new forms—from very simple forms to more advanced forms. You can use Design View, add fields to the form, and build the form manually. When relationships exist between tables in a database, Access is able to display related data when you open the table datasheet. In many cases, Access analyzes the relationship between the tables so that you can access data located in the related table from the main table.

┌The expand/collapse button displays/hides related data.

	Customer ID	First Name	Last Name	Address
⊞	ADA001	NATE	ADAMS	3037 WELLS FARGO DRIVE
⊞	ADA002	DEANNA	ADAMS	1412 REDWOOD
⊞	ALB001	BETTY	ALBURN	264 W PROSPECT ROAD
⊟	ALS001	PATRICK	ALSTAD	1309 CENTENNIAL

Each row in the parent table represent a record.

OrderID	Inventory Numb	OrderDate	Quantity	Click to Add
iJ-13	DVD	8/1/2011	1	
* (New)			0	

Data from a related table displays as a subset datasheet.

| ⊞ | BAK001 | DARRELL | BAKER | 2519 EASTWOOD DRIVE |

Removing the Layout

When you create a form using the Form button on the Ribbon or using the Form Wizard, Access positions fields according to the layout you choose. Because of this layout format, selecting individual controls and arranging the controls on the form can be a challenge. You can remove the layout Access applies by displaying the form in Design View and choosing Arrange→Table→Remove Layout on the Ribbon.

Connecting Related Tables in Forms

Establishing relationships among database tables also enables Access to display table data on forms along with a subset of data from a related table. When relationships are established, Access creates the *main form* from data contained in the table or query on which you base the form and places related data in a *subform* on the main form. Subforms are simply subsets of data from the related table shown within the form. In online help, Access refers to the main form as the *parent* and the subform as the *child*. You can add multiple subforms to main forms when all data comes from related tables.

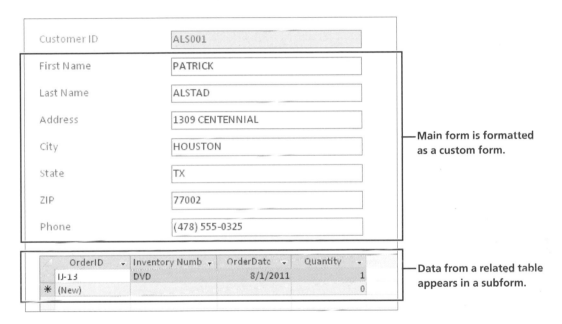

Main form is formatted as a custom form.

Data from a related table appears in a subform.

Creating a Form with Subform

After relationships are established in a database, creating a standard form using the Create→ Forms→Form command on the Ribbon automatically creates a main form with a subform. The subform displays data from a related table created by a lookup field. In addition, Access provides different techniques for creating forms that contain a subform. You can use the Form Wizard to create the form with the subform. You can also custom design your own form and add a subform control.

Using the Form Wizard

Using the Form Wizard, Access prompts you to select the related tables or queries containing fields to include on the form and then prompts you to identify whether you want to create a form with a subform or if you want to link the data from the subform to the main form. To make the data more accessible, creating a form with a subform makes data entry more efficient.

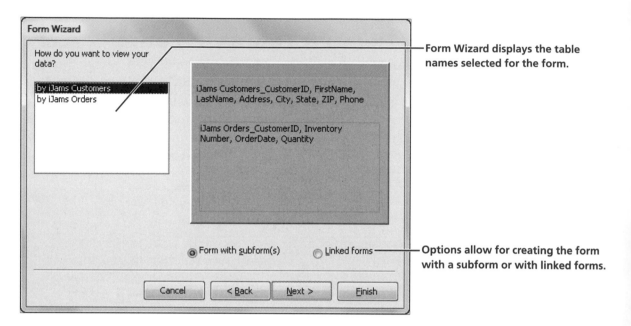

Form Wizard displays the table names selected for the form.

Options allow for creating the form with a subform or with linked forms.

Using the Subform Control

When you custom design a form or when you want to add a subform to an existing form, you can add the subform using the Subform control. Using this tool enables you to size the control to fit the area of the main form you want it to occupy. Access places an unbound control on the main form and then you set the table or query from which you want Access to draw related records.

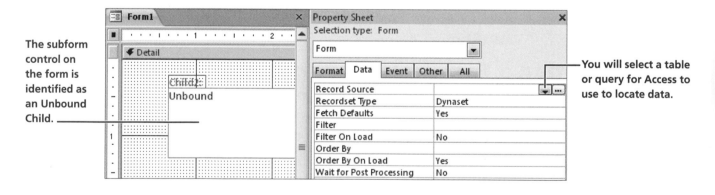

The subform control on the form is identified as an Unbound Child.

You will select a table or query for Access to use to locate data.

Task	Procedure
Use the wizard to create a form with a subform	■ Choose Create→Forms→Form Wizard [icon] on the Ribbon. ■ Work through the wizard screens.
Add a subform to a form	■ Create a main form. ■ Choose Design→Controls→Subform/Subreport [icon] on the Ribbon. ■ Draw a control on the main form of the appropriate size and in the appropriate position. ■ Display the Property Sheet and set the Source Object property on the Data tab to identify the data source.

DEVELOP YOUR SKILLS 9.2.1

Create a Form Containing a Subform

In this exercise, you will use the Form Wizard to create and save a form that contains a subform to display data from a related table.

1. **Open** the iJams database from the Lesson 09 folder and **save** the file as a new database named **iJams Forms**.

2. Choose **Create→Forms→Form Wizard** [icon] on the Ribbon to launch the Form Wizard.

3. Follow these steps to select fields from the first table:

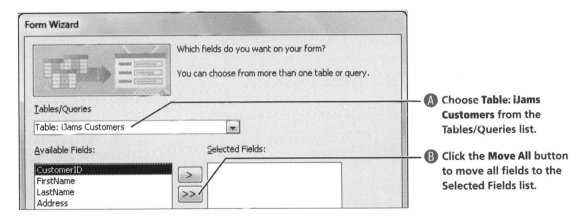

4. Follow these steps to select fields from the related table:

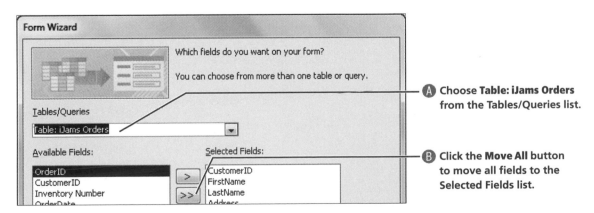

5. Click **Next** and review the arrangement of data as a form with subform.

6. Click **Next** to accept the default settings for the form and review the format for the subform.

7. Ensure that **Datasheet** format is selected for the layout of the subform and click **Next**.

8. Follow these steps to complete the form:

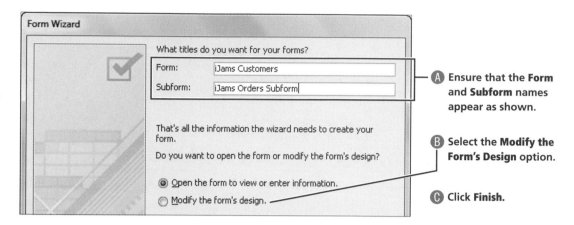

Ⓐ Ensure that the **Form** and **Subform** names appear as shown.

Ⓑ Select the **Modify the Form's Design** option.

Ⓒ Click **Finish**.

Access saves the form and opens the form in Design View.

9. Compare your form to the following illustration:

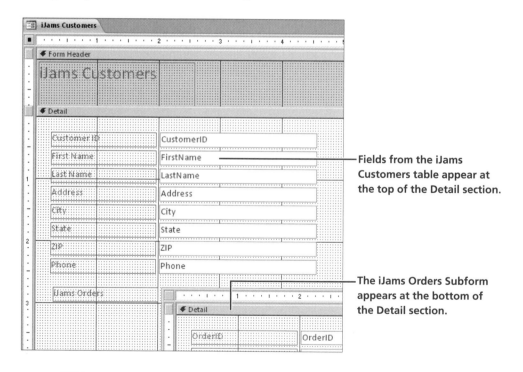

Fields from the iJams Customers table appear at the top of the Detail section.

The iJams Orders Subform appears at the bottom of the Detail section.

10. **Close** ☒ the form.

Editing a Data Source

Video Lesson   labyrinthelab.com/videos

Each table or query used in a form, whether the data is displayed in the main form or in a subform, is called the *record source* because the table or query displays the data in the form. When you create a form that contains a subform, Access actually creates two forms and displays both forms in the Navigation Pane—one for the main form and another for the subform. Access identifies the subform by including the word *subform* in the form name. Each form has a separate record source—in this case, a table—from which it gets data.

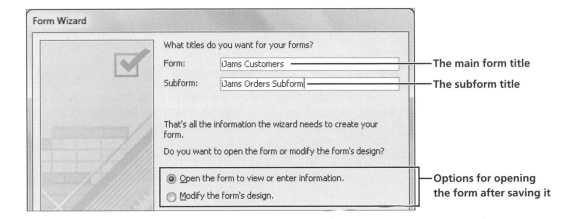

The main form title — iJams Customers

The subform title — iJams Orders Subform

Options for opening the form after saving it

Analyzing the iJams Orders Subform Record Source

Form properties display the record source for each form in an Access database. As a result, you can identify the record source for the main form and the subform by displaying the Property Sheet.

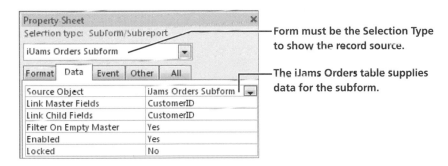

Form must be the Selection Type to show the record source.

The iJams Orders table supplies data for the subform.

Because data entry personnel often use a Customer form to process customer orders, you want the form to calculate a total for each item ordered and a grand total for all items ordered. This information is unavailable from the iJams Orders table. However, the Order Processing query contains the required fields for setting up the calculations you need. As a result, you can create a separate form using the Order Processing query and reset the record source for the subform to access data from the new form.

Identifying Form Design Features

As a refresher, the major elements and controls found in the form Design window include:

Form Sections	Description
Sections	The major parts of the form, such as the Form Header, the Form Footer, the Detail, the Page Header, and the Page Footer. Section bars divide form sections.
Form Header/Footer	The sections of a form that contain text, pictures, and other items that are repeated at the top (header) or bottom (footer) of each form.
Detail section	The main section of the form that normally displays data from database tables that varies from record to record.
Page Header/Footer	The sections of a form that contain text and other items that are repeated at the top (header) or bottom (footer) of every *printed page*.

Form Controls	Description
Controls	Items on a form or report page that display data, perform actions, and decorate the form. Access uses three main types of controls on forms—bound controls, unbound controls, and calculated controls. Each control consists of two parts—control label and control text box—that are tied to a field in a database table.
Bound control	A control that ties, or binds, data displayed on a form to a field in a database table so that the field value appears on the form. Bound controls normally appear in the Detail section of a form.
Unbound control	An item on a form that is independent of data and fields in a database table. Unbound controls can be lines, rectangles, pictures, and so forth. Unbound controls can appear in any form section.
Calculated control	A control that is tied to an expression or calculated field constructed in a query. Calculated controls normally appear in the Detail or Form Footer section of the form.
Control label	The part of a control that contains text to identify the data displayed on the form. Normally, the control label text is the field name or caption set for the field. For example, *Customer Number* is a label that identifies the *Customer#* field.
Control text box	The part of a control that displays data from a field in an Access table. For example, *TC-1001* is the data contained in the *Order#* field.

DEVELOP YOUR SKILLS 9.2.2

Create a Form and Change a Record Source

In this exercise, you will create another new form based on the Order Processing query and set it as the data source for the subform in the iJams Customers form.

1. Click the **Order Processing** query on the Navigation Pane to select it (but do not open it).

2. Choose **Create→Forms→Form** on the Ribbon to create a form using all fields in the query.

3. **Save** the form using the form name **Order Processing**.

4. Display the form in **Form Design View**.

5. **Press** F4 to display the Property Sheet and then follow these steps to reformat the new form:

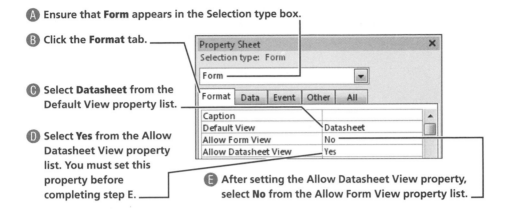

Ⓐ Ensure that **Form** appears in the Selection type box.

Ⓑ Click the **Format** tab.

Ⓒ Select **Datasheet** from the Default View property list.

Ⓓ Select **Yes** from the Allow Datasheet View property list. You must set this property before completing step E.

Ⓔ After setting the Allow Datasheet View property, select **No** from the Allow Form View property list.

Property Sheet

Selection type: Form

Form

Format	Data	Event	Other	All

Caption	
Default View	Datasheet
Allow Form View	No
Allow Datasheet View	Yes

Although you have set new properties, Access only displays the default view when you open the form.

6. **Save** 🖫 the form and **close** ✖ it. Then **open** the form again to display the datasheet.

Change the Subform Source Object

7. **Right-click** the iJams Customers form and choose **Design View.**

8. **Press** F4 to display the Property Sheet, if it is closed, and then follow these steps to change the data source for the subform control:

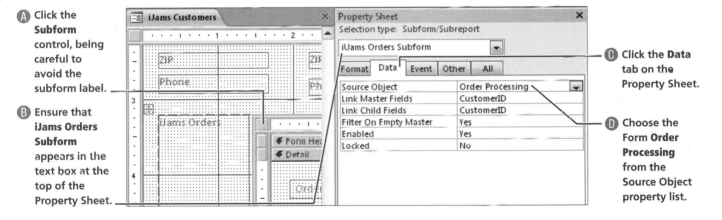

Ⓐ Click the **Subform** control, being careful to avoid the subform label.

Ⓑ Ensure that **iJams Orders Subform** appears in the text box at the top of the Property Sheet.

Ⓒ Click the **Data** tab on the Property Sheet.

Ⓓ Choose the Form **Order Processing** from the Source Object property list.

Property Sheet

Selection type: Subform/Subreport

iJams Orders Subform

Format	Data	Event	Other	All

Source Object	Order Processing
Link Master Fields	CustomerID
Link Child Fields	CustomerID
Filter On Empty Master	Yes
Enabled	Yes
Locked	No

Access reformats the subform control on the main form to display data from the Order Processing form. Notice, when you display the drop-down list of source objects, that Access identifies objects by type such as Table and Query.

9. **Save** 🖫 and **close** ✖ the form.

Test the Source Change

Now that you have a new data source, you will test it to ensure that it is accurate.

10. **Open** the iJams Customers form, navigate to **record 14** to view the orders displayed in the subform, and compare your form to the one shown.
    Only orders for specific customers appear when their record is displayed.

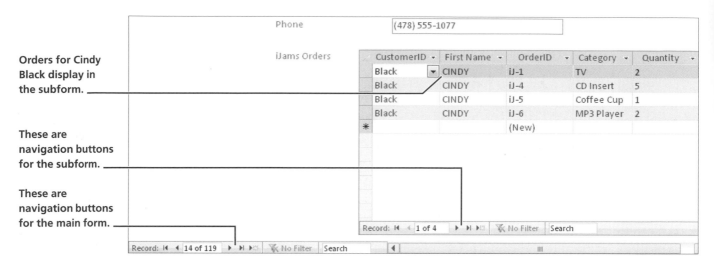

Orders for Cindy Black display in the subform.

These are navigation buttons for the subform.

These are navigation buttons for the main form.

11. **Close** the form, **saving** changes if prompted.

Formatting a Form

Video Lesson   labyrinthelab.com/videos

When you create a new form using the Simple Form tool or using the Form Wizard, Access places all fields from the selected table or query on the form and arranges them following a pre-designed generic layout. You can then display the form in Design View and edit the form by modifying the field arrangement, editing labels, sizing boxes that display data, or modifying the form properties, as you did in the last exercise. You can also use features available in Access to modify a form style and insert graphics to enhance visual elements.

When a form contains a subform, you can use the same techniques to modify the subform directly on the main form or open the subform separately and make changes to the form.

Tips for Working with Controls

You should already be familiar with techniques for moving, sizing, adding, deleting, and formatting form controls. As you know, selecting, moving, positioning, and aligning each form control individually can be tedious and time-consuming. You can move selected controls by dragging them or by pressing the arrow keys on the keyboard. However, positioning the controls precisely where you want them can be a challenge, and distributing controls evenly across a space is equally challenging. Fortunately, Access contains alignment and distribution options that enable you to accomplish these tasks more easily. Try these techniques when you have trouble positioning a control in just the right spot on a form. And don't forget the Undo feature—it's a handy tool for reversing actions, restoring controls deleted in error, and correcting other mistakes!

Task	Procedure
Align controls	■ Select all controls you want to align. ■ Choose Arrange→Sizing & Ordering→Align on the Ribbon and click the appropriate alignment button.
Nudge controls into position	■ Select the control you want to position. ■ Press and hold the Ctrl key and tap the arrow keys to nudge a control into place.
Distribute controls equally	■ Select the controls to distribute. ■ Choose Arrange→Sizing & Ordering→Size/Space on the Ribbon and click the appropriate button to make horizontal or vertical spacing equal.
Increase or decrease control spacing	■ Select the controls for which you want to adjust spacing. ■ Choose Arrange→Sizing & Ordering→Size/Space on the Ribbon and click the button to increase or decrease horizontal or vertical spacing or to set equal spacing.
Size controls equally	■ Select the controls you want to size. ■ Choose Arrange→Sizing & Ordering→Size/Space on the Ribbon and click the button to size the controls to tallest, shortest, widest, narrowest, or to fit the longest entry.

Using the Table Selection Button

If you have used the table feature in Microsoft Word, you may already be familiar with the table selection button. The table selection button appears in the upper-left corner outside the top row of the table and enables you to select the entire table when you click the button. With the entire table selected, you can then move and position all table or field columns at the same time.

Format the Form

In this exercise, you will modify the iJams Customers form by deleting, moving, and sizing controls, changing control label captions, and adding a graphic and title to the form.

Before You Begin: Your iJams Forms database should be open.

1. Display the iJams Customers form in **Design View,** collapse the **Navigation Pane,** and close the **Property Sheet.**

2. Follow these steps to resize the form and display the Form Header section:

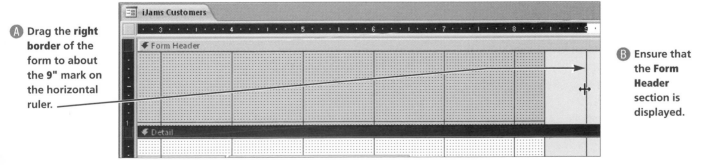

Ⓐ Drag the **right border** of the form to about the 9" mark on the horizontal ruler.

Ⓑ Ensure that the **Form Header** section is displayed.

3. Scroll down the form until the **subform control** comes into view.

4. Select each of the following controls in the subform and **press** ⌐Delete⌐ to remove the field from the subform: FirstName, CustomerID.

5. Follow these steps to reposition the customer data on the main form:

Ⓐ Select **all controls** in the main form.

Ⓑ **Drag** any selected control to the **right** to position all controls in the approximate center of the form.

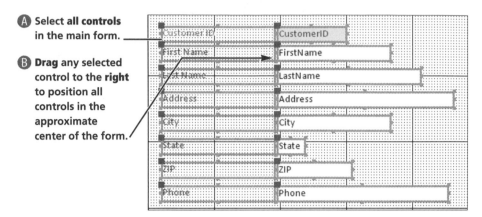

Size the Subform Control

6. Follow these steps to size the subform control:

Ⓐ Click the subform control to select it.

Ⓑ Drag the **right border** of the control to almost the edge of the window.

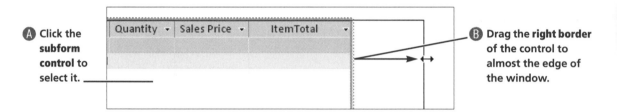

7. Switch to **Layout View** ▦ and **double-click** the right border of each subform column heading to size the columns and size the control to display all columns.

8. **Save** 💾 changes to the form and switch back to **Design View.**

9. Click the **OrderID** control label in the subform and display the **Property Sheet**.

10. Change the **Caption** property for OrderID in the *Subform* to `Order Number`.

Add a Title to the Form

11. Select the title in the **Form Header** section.

12. Choose **Format→Font→Font Color** 🅰 menu ▾ on the Ribbon and choose **white.**

13. Choose **Format→Font→Font Size** on the Ribbon, type **38**, and then **press** ⌐Enter⌐.

14. Follow these steps to position and size the title control:

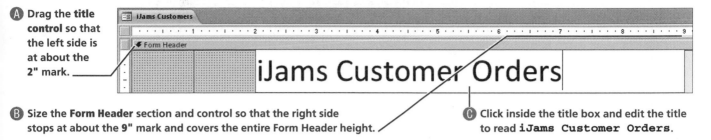

Ⓐ Drag the **title control** so that the left side is at about the 2" mark.

Ⓑ Size the **Form Header** section and control so that the right side stops at about the 9" mark and covers the entire Form Header height.

Ⓒ Click inside the title box and edit the title to read `iJams Customer Orders`.

Add a Logo to the Form

15. Choose **Design→Header/Footer→Logo** 🖼 on the Ribbon and **double-click** the iJams.bmp file in the Lesson 09 folder.
    Access adds the logo to the Form Header.

16. **Delete** the attached title box on the right side of the logo; then **save** and **adjust** the position of the logo and title controls in the Form Header.

17. **Save** 💾 and **close** ✖ the form.

9.3 Adding a Calculated Control to a Form

Video Lesson   labyrinthelab.com/videos

As you know, you can create calculated fields in queries and add calculated controls to forms and reports. Calculated fields in queries are given a specific name followed by the fields containing the values on which you want Access to perform a calculation. Calculated controls, on the other hand, are constructed on forms or reports using an *unbound control* to which you add the formula for the calculation. No name is associated with these controls.

Totaling Calculated Fields

Each field used in an equation on an Access database object requires an identity or name. In most cases, the field name is used in equations. This is true of calculated fields you create in queries. Controls on forms or reports have no identity of their own that you can reference in other calculated fields. Therefore, if you want to calculate a sum or average of calculated fields, you must first create the calculated field in a query so that you can assign a name to the field. By using the query as the data source for the form, you can then reference the calculated field in other calculations you add to unbound controls on forms.

For example, suppose you want to show a total of an invoice you are sending to a customer. The total for each item has been added to the order, but the order total, tax, and shipping charges are not. You can add calculated controls to the invoice to total all items ordered.

Positioning Calculated Controls in Form Sections

The position of the calculated control determines how Access performs the calculation:

- Calculated controls in the Detail section calculate the values that appear for each record in the form each time you open the form.

- Calculated controls in a subform calculate values that appear for each record in the subform.

- Calculated controls found in the Form Footer or Page Footer sections calculate totals and other operations using aggregate functions.

Applying Totals to Datasheets

When the form you are designing displays data in datasheet format, adding calculated controls to a form fails to display the data as you intend for it to. As a result, when you are displaying data in a subform using Datasheet format, you should add the totals of the costs using the Totals feature in Access. You may recall that the Totals feature appears on the Home→Records group on the Ribbon.

Using the Expression Builder

You can create a calculated control by typing control field names and operators (multiply, divide, add, subtract, etc.) directly in the Control Source property in the properties box. However, many people consider using the Expression Builder dialog box an easier way to build an expression. The Expression Builder dialog box contains features that enable you to paste field names and operators required for the expression right in the dialog box so that you can review the expression. You can use the Expression Builder to create expressions in queries, on forms, or on reports when other tools are inappropriate, such as when a calculation needs to be performed to add tax or shipping to a form.

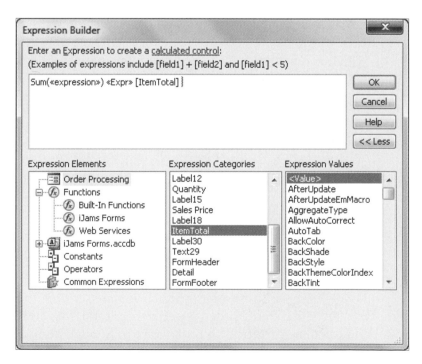

The Expression Builder dialog box contains tools for creating calculated controls.

Add Totals to the Subform Datasheet

In this exercise, you will use the Totals feature in Access to total each customer's order in the subform.

1. **Double-click** the Order Processing form in the iJams Forms database.

2. Choose **Home→Records→Totals** Σ to add totals to the datasheet.

3. Click the **ItemTotal** column on the Total row and choose **Sum** from the drop-down list.

4. **Close** the form, **saving** changes if prompted.

5. **Open** the iJams Customers form and display record 14.

6. Compare the subform on screen to the subform shown here, noting the total at the bottom of the order list:

iJams Orders	Order Nu ⌄	Category ⌄	Quantity ⌄	Sales Price ⌄	ItemTotal ⌄
	iJ-1	TV	2	$595.00	$1,190.00
	iJ-4	CD Insert	5	$5.00	$25.00
	iJ-5	Coffee Cup	1	$10.00	$10.00
	iJ-6	MP3 Player	2	$375.00	$750.00
*	(New)				
		Total			$1,975.00

7. **Close** the form, **saving** changes if prompted.

Adding the Current Date to the Form

Video Lesson   labyrinthelab.com/videos

Each time you open a form, Access updates the information on the form to reflect changes since the last time you viewed it. Because data contained in a database changes constantly and forms are printed regularly, keeping track of the most current printed data is important. You can add a date and/or time to a form to help you track them. Most businesses display the current date in the Form Header or Form Footer section. Access places the date and time in the Form Header section, but you can move the information to other form sections.

Add the Current Date to a Form

In this exercise, you will add the date to the iJams Customers *form, and then move it to the Form Footer section.*

1. Display the iJams Customers form in **Design View**.

2. Choose **Design→Header/Footer→Date & Time** 🖼 on the Ribbon to open the Date and Time dialog box.

3. Follow these steps to set options in the Date and Time dialog box:

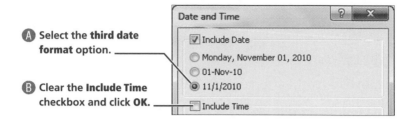

Ⓐ Select the **third date format** option. ⎯⎯⎯

Ⓑ Clear the **Include Time** checkbox and click **OK.** ⎯⎯

Access places the control in the Form Header section of the form.

4. Follow these steps to drag the Date control to the Form Footer section:

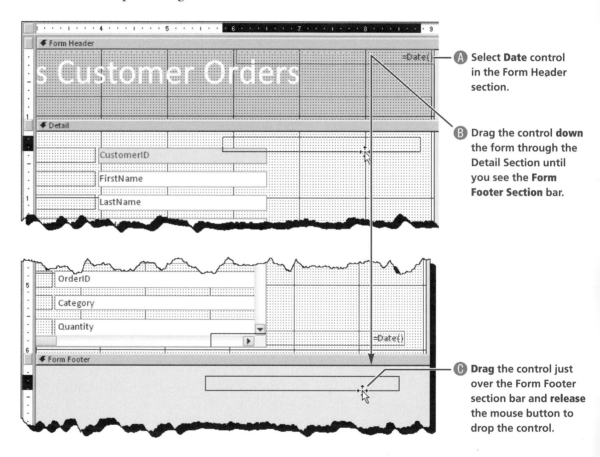

Ⓐ Select **Date** control in the Form Header section.

Ⓑ Drag the control **down** the form through the Detail Section until you see the **Form Footer Section** bar.

Ⓒ **Drag** the control just over the Form Footer section bar and **release** the mouse button to drop the control.

Access expands the Form Footer section to accommodate the date control.

5. **Save** changes to the form, view the form in Form view, and then **close** it.

9.4 Setting Properties to Assist and Control Data Entry

Video Lesson labyrinthelab.com/videos

You have already used many of the properties available in the Property Sheet and have also noticed the different properties available for different types of controls. Some of these properties help you control or limit data entry, while other properties assist you with data entry. These properties are identified in this section.

Disabling Form Fields

In some circumstances, the fields on a form reflect data that users do not enter and/or should not enter or edit. Many forms also contain settings that enter default values such as states or values such as cities that correspond to data contained in fields such as ZIP codes. To protect fields on a form from editing or data entry or to skip fields as you enter new data, you can *disable* the field in the Property Sheet. Disabled fields are inaccessible for data entry. When a field is disabled, it appears grayed out and is not accessible to the user. During data entry, Access skips disabled fields and moves directly to the first field on a form that is enabled and accessible.

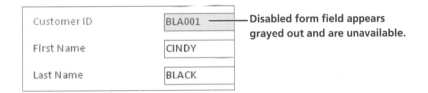
Disabled form field appears grayed out and are unavailable.

Locking Form Fields

Another way to protect fields from being edited is by *locking* the field. The advantage of locking the field is that it appears available on the form. It is accessible to the user, but when the user tries to change the data, Access prevents data editing. Many people prefer locking fields because they appear properly when a form is printed—the grayed out appearance of disabled fields prints faintly. To lock a field, set the Locked property to Yes.

Locked form fields are available but refuse edits.

QUICK REFERENCE	DISABLING AND LOCKING FORM FIELDS
Task	**Procedure**
Disable a field	■ Display the form containing the control in Design View and display the Property Sheet. ■ Select the control you want to disable and set the Enabled property on the Data tab to No.
Lock a field	■ Display the form containing the control in Design View and display the Property Sheet. ■ Select the control you want to lock and set the Locked property on the Data tab to Yes.

Disable and Lock Form Fields

In this exercise, you will disable the CustomerID field in the main form and the OrderID field in the subform in the iJams Customers form to make them unavailable. In addition, you will lock the Sales Price field in the subform so that it cannot be edited.

Before You Begin: Your iJams Forms database should be open.

1. Display the iJams Customers form in **Design View** and display the **Property Sheet**.

2. Click the **CustomerID** control text box on the main form and then click the **Property Sheet Data** tab.

3. Change the Enabled property to **No.**

4. Repeat the procedures outlined in **steps 2 and 3** to disable the OrderID control text box in the subform.

5. Click the **Sales Price** control text box in the subform and set the Locked property to **Yes.**

Test the Property Settings

6. Switch to **Form View,** display record **4,** and compare the form to the following illustration.

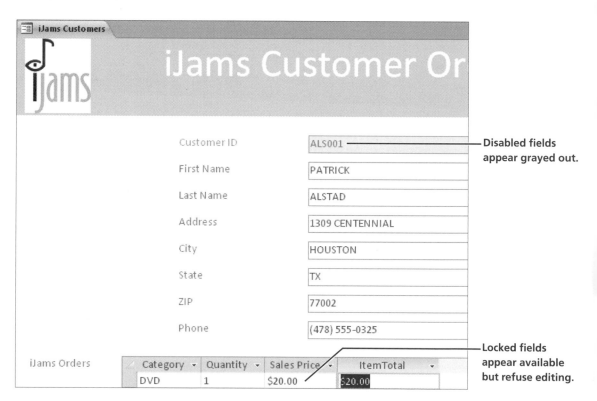

7. Try to edit the sales price for one of the items in the subform.

8. **Save** and **close** the form.

Adding Tips to Controls

Video Lesson   labyrinthelab.com/videos

When you create a database table and define each field, you have the opportunity to enter a description of the field in the Description column. Text you type in the Description field column of table Design View appears in the status bar when the field is active during data entry. These descriptions also appear in the status bar when a table field appears on a form. Although forms identify most data by including field control labels, sometimes the labels for specific fields such as State and ZIP are removed from a form when the controls are grouped together under a more general label such as Address. To help data entry personnel determine what data to type in a field, you can add additional tips to display onscreen by setting the ControlTip Text property for a control. Text you add to the ControlTip Text property appears as a ScreenTip when the user points to a field control. Setting ScreenTips helps to eliminate confusion associated with unlabeled controls and provides explanations for other controls.

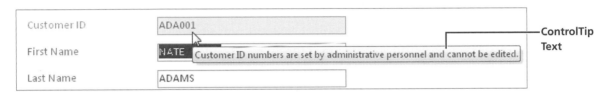

DEVELOP YOUR SKILLS 9.4.2
Create Control ScreenTips

In this exercise, you will create ScreenTips for the disabled and locked fields on the iJams Customers *form to explain why they are inaccessible.*

Before You Begin: Your iJams Forms database should be open.

1. Display the iJams Customers form in **Design View** and display the **Property Sheet.**

2. Click the **CustomerID** control text box and then click the **Property Sheet Other** tab.

3. Locate the **ControlTip Text** property and type the following text into the property:

   `Customer ID numbers are set by administrative personnel and cannot be edited.`

4. Repeat the procedures outlined in **steps 2 and 3** to enter the following text for the subform controls identified:

Control	ControlTip Text
OrderID Text Box	The system generates order numbers. They cannot be edited.
Sales Price	Sales price values cannot be changed.

View the ScreenTips

5. **Save** the form and then switch to **Form View.**

6. Point to the **Customer ID** field on the form and review the ScreenTip.

Customer ID	ADA001
First Name	

Customer ID numbers are set by administrative personnel and cannot be edited.

Tips for the subform fields display when the subform is open outside of the main form.

Creating a Pop-up Form

Video Lesson labyrinthelab.com/videos

Both forms and reports can be set to open as pop-up windows that stay on top of other open database objects. They can be set to prompt a user for information or to display a window containing supplemental data while allowing the user full access to the database window and other database objects. Such forms or reports can help data entry personnel look up data entry values when they are processing orders or looking up the price of an item. You can apply different formats for pop-up windows you create in Access.

Modeless pop-up forms sit on top of other forms so that you can continue to work.

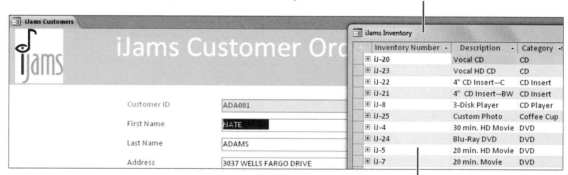

Pop-up forms are formatted as separate windows rather than tabbed forms.

QUICK REFERENCE	IDENTIFYING POP-UP WINDOW MODES
Mode	**Description**
Modeless Pop-Up	Creates a pop-up that sits on top of other open windows in such a way that you can continue to work in the database while it is open. For example, when you are processing orders, you could set the Inventory List to open as a modeless pop-up to ensure that you have the correct inventory number.
Modal Pop-Up	Operates as a custom dialog box that prevents you from accessing other database objects while it is open. They call for action that is required before you can continue.

Create a Pop-Up Form

In this exercise, you will format the iJams Inventory form as a pop-up form by editing the form properties and then you will test the settings.

Before You Begin: Your iJams Forms database should be open.

1. **Select** the iJams Inventory table and choose **Create→Forms→Form** to create a new form and **save** the form as **iJams Inventory**.

2. Display the iJams Inventory form in **Design View** and display the **Property Sheet**.

3. Click the **Property Sheet Other** tab and set the Pop Up property to **Yes.**

4. Click the **Property Sheet Format** tab and set the Default View property to **Datasheet;** then set the Allow Datasheet View to **Yes.**

5. **Save** and **close** the form.

Test the Property Setting

6. Open the **iJams Customers** form and then open the **Inventory** form.

7. Close the **Navigation Pane** and follow these steps to test the pop-up:

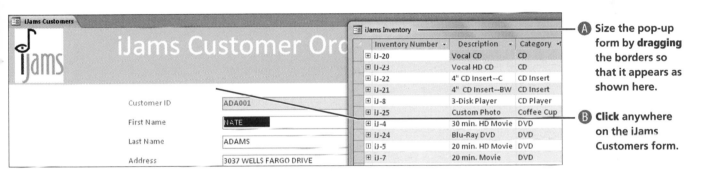

Ⓐ Size the pop-up form by **dragging** the borders so that it appears as shown here.

Ⓑ **Click** anywhere on the iJams Customers form.

The pop-up form remains on top and available as a reference as you work in other forms.

8. **Close** the iJams Inventory form.

Hiding Form Screen Elements

Video Lesson   labyrinthelab.com/videos

When form data fits onscreen within the screen size of most monitors, you may want to hide the record selector bars and scroll bars so that the form presents a better onscreen appearance. These onscreen elements are controlled by form properties.

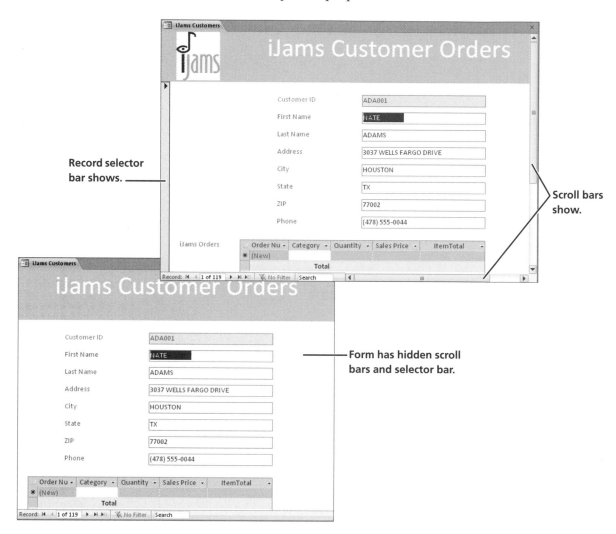

Record selector bar shows.

Scroll bars show.

Form has hidden scroll bars and selector bar.

QUICK REFERENCE	SETTING FORM SCREEN ELEMENT PROPERTIES
Task	**Procedure**
Add control ScreenTips	■ Display the form containing the control in Design View and display the Property Sheet.
	■ Select the control to contain the ScreenTip and click the Property Sheet Other tab.
	■ Type the text to display in the ControlTip Text property.
Create a modeless pop-up form	■ Display the form you want to change in Design View and display the Property Sheet.
	■ Click the Property Sheet Other tab.
	■ Set the Pop Up property to Yes.

Task	Procedure
Create a modal pop-up form	■ Display the form you want to change in Design View and display the Property Sheet. ■ Click the Property Sheet Other tab. ■ Set the Pop Up property to Yes and set the Modal property to Yes.
Hide the form record selector	■ Display the form you want to change in Design View and display the Property Sheet. ■ Click the Property Sheet Format tab. ■ Set the Record Selectors property to No.
Hide form scroll bars	■ Display the form you want to change in Design View and display the Property Sheet. ■ Click the Property Sheet Format tab. ■ Set the Scroll Bars property to No.
Select a record when the record selector is hidden	■ Display the record onscreen. ■ Press [Shift]+[Spacebar] to select it.

DEVELOP YOUR SKILLS 9.4.4

Hide Form Record Selector and Scroll Bars

In this exercise, you will hide the record selector bar and scroll bars for the iJams Customers form.

Before You Begin: Your iJams Forms database should be open.

1. Display the iJams Customers form in **Design View** and display the **Property Sheet.**

2. Follow these steps to hide the screen elements:

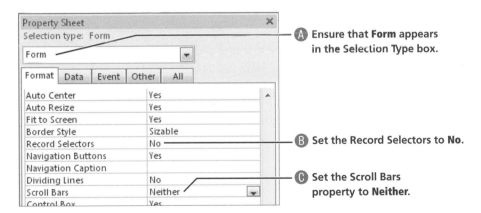

Ⓐ Ensure that **Form** appears in the Selection Type box.

Ⓑ Set the Record Selectors to **No.**

Ⓒ Set the Scroll Bars property to **Neither.**

3. **Save** 💾 changes to the form and then display it in **Form View.**

4. Compare the form to the following illustration.

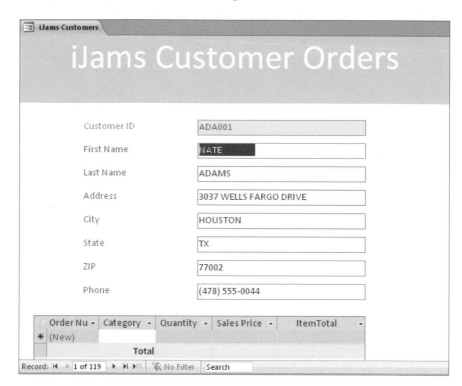

Depending on your screen resolution and size, your form may look different.

5. Close ☒ all open database objects, **close** the database, and **exit** Access.

9.5 Concepts Review

Concepts Review   labyrinthelab.com/acc10

To check your knowledge of the key concepts introduced in this lesson, complete the Concepts Review quiz by going to the URL listed above. If your classroom is using Labyrinth eLab, you may complete the Concepts Review quiz from within your eLab course.

Reinforce Your Skills

Create a Form

The State of Oklahoma is developing a database for Oklahoma drivers. Data entry personnel who enter data into each state database have varying levels of knowledge about databases. As a result, they need a user-friendly form to make it easier to enter data. The form you create contains fields from multiple tables in the database that enable users to display and enter insurance data for drivers. Because relationships have been established among database tables, you can create the form using the Forms Wizard feature so that Access creates the subform. In this exercise, you will create the first draft of the form.

1. **Launch** Access and **open** the rs-Oklahoma Drivers database from the Lesson 09 folder. Create a **backup** of the database named **rs-OK Driver Forms**.

2. Open the **Navigation Pane** and select (but do not open) the Test Drivers table.

3. Choose **Create→Forms→Form Wizard** 🖳 on the Ribbon.

4. Move the following fields to the Selected Fields list: DriverID, FirstName, LastName, Street, City, State, ZIP, ExpirationDate, and DateOfBirth.

5. Follow these steps to complete the list of fields to include in the form:

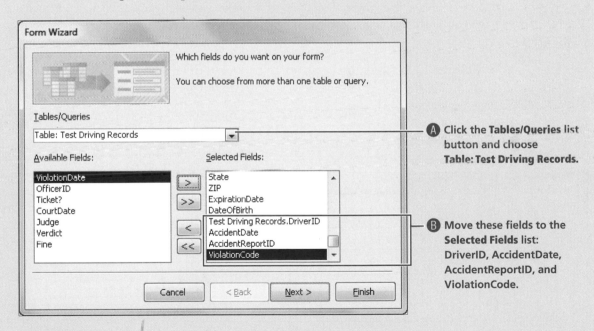

Ⓐ Click the **Tables/Queries** list button and choose **Table: Test Driving Records.**

Ⓑ Move these fields to the **Selected Fields** list: **DriverID, AccidentDate, AccidentReportID,** and **ViolationCode.**

6. Click **Next,** select the **Form with subform(s) option,** and set the view to by **TestDrivers.**

7. Click **Next** and select the **Datasheet layout.**

8. Click **Next** and click **Finish.**
   Access opens the form in Form View.

9. **Save** 💾 and **close** ⊠ the form.

Arrange and Size Form Controls

The basic form you created in the last exercise is ready for some modification to organize and size the fields more appropriately. In this exercise, you will modify the form layout and size controls to display data.

Before You Begin: *Your rs-OK Driver Forms database should be open.*

1. Display the Test Drivers form in **Design View**.

2. Drag the **right border** of the form to about the **8″** mark on the horizontal ruler.

3. Follow these steps to adjust the layout of the form controls:

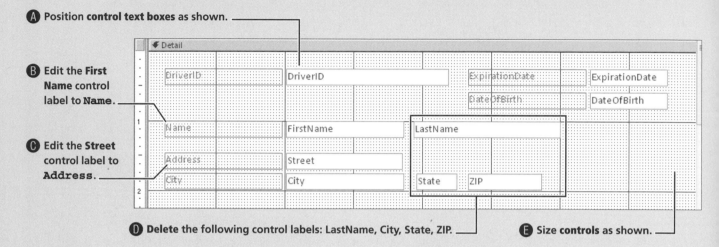

Ⓐ Position **control text boxes** as shown.

Ⓑ Edit the **First Name** control label to **Name**.

Ⓒ Edit the **Street** control label to **Address**.

Ⓓ Delete the following control labels: LastName, City, State, ZIP.

Ⓔ Size **controls** as shown.

4. Follow these steps to align and distribute controls by selecting groups of controls and clicking the appropriate Control Size or Control Alignment button:

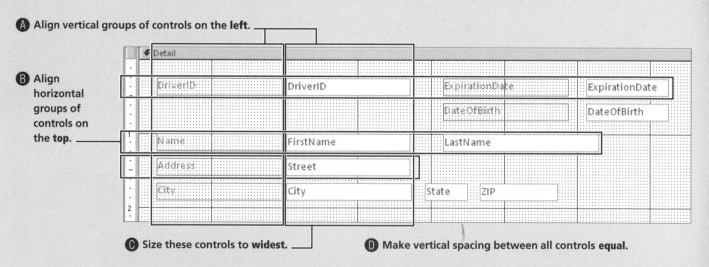

Ⓐ Align vertical groups of controls on the **left**.

Ⓑ Align horizontal groups of controls on the top.

Ⓒ Size these controls to **widest**.

Ⓓ Make vertical spacing between all controls **equal**.

5. **Save** 💾 changes to the form and then switch to **Form View**.

6. **Print** a copy of the first record form and then **close** ❎ the form.

Add Date Control to a Form and Edit Captions and Title

The form you are developing needs a date as well as control tips for some of the controls. In this exercise, you will add a date control, edit the title, adjust the size of the columns in the subform, and set control captions.

Before You Begin: *Your rs-OK Driver Forms database should be open.*

1. Display the Test Drivers form in **Design View** and display the **Property Sheet.**

2. Set the **Caption** property for each of the following control labels as shown in the following table:

Old Label	New Label
DateOfBirth	Date of Birth
ExpirationDate	Expiration Date

3. Follow these steps to change the text that will appear in the form tab:

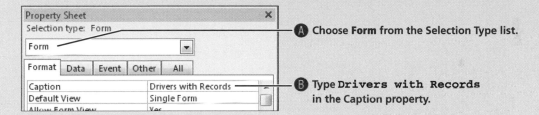

Ⓐ Choose **Form** from the Selection Type list.

Ⓑ Type **Drivers with Records** in the Caption property.

The caption will appear only when the form is displayed in Form or Layout View. The name in the Form Header section does not change.

4. Click the **Test Drivers** title in the Form Header and change the caption to **Drivers with Records.**

5. Set the following properties on the Format tab for the title control:

Property	Setting
Fore Color	Access Theme 8
Font Size	36
Font Weight	Medium

6. Adjust the size of the title control to display all text on **one line.**

7. Choose **Design→Header/Footer→Date & Time** 🗓 on the Ribbon to open the Date and Time dialog box.

8. Check the **Include Date** checkbox, select the **second** date format, and clear the checkmark from the **Include Time** checkbox.

9. Click **OK** to add the Date control to the form and then drag the **Date** control from the Form Header section to the **Form Footer** section.

10. **Save** 🖫 the form and all form objects and then display the form in **Layout View.**

11. Adjust the size of the **datasheet columns** in the subform to more appropriately fit the data and then size the subform control to display all columns.

12. **Save** 🖫 the form and then **print** a copy of the first record.

Add Control Tips and Set Control Properties

The form you are developing will potentially be used by field personnel to retrieve data. Therefore, there are a number of controls that should be locked and disabled. In addition, you can remove the screen elements from the form because the entire form will appear onscreen when field personnel call it up. In this exercise, you will set properties to control these features and add control tips.

Before You Begin: Your rs-OK Driver Forms database should be open.

1. Display the Test Drivers form in **Design View** and display the **Property Sheet**.

2. Click the **Other** tab on the Property Sheet and set the following tips in the ControlTip Text property for associated controls:

Control	ControlTip Text
Street text box	Type the street address.
City text box	Type the city name.
State text box	Type the 2-letter state abbreviation.
ZIP text box	Type the ZIP code.

3. Set the Enabled property on the Data tab to **No** for the following fields: DriverID in the main form and subform.

4. Set the Locked property on the Data tab to **Yes** for the following fields: DateOfBirth, AccidentDate, AccidentReportID, ViolationCode.

5. Click the **Detail** section bar on the main form, choose **Form** from the Selection type box at the top of the Property Sheet, and set the Scroll Bars property on the Format tab to **Neither.**

6. Set the Record Selectors property to **No.**

7. **Save** 🖫 the form, display it in **Form View,** and then **print** a copy of the form.

Create a Calculated Form Control

The database is currently set up to enter only the issue date of drivers licenses. Expiration dates will be generated using a calculated field. Each license is good for five years from the month of issue. In this exercise, you will create a calculated control that calculates the expiration year automatically by adding five years to the issue date.

Before You Begin: Your rs-OK Driver Forms database should be open.

1. Display the Test Drivers form in **Design View** and display the **Property Sheet.**

2. Select the **ExpirationDate** control text box and then click the **Property Sheet Data** tab.

3. Click the **Control Source** property box and then click the **Build** button to open the Expression Builder.

4. **Delete** the field name in the box at the top of the Expression Builder and then follow these steps to start the expression:

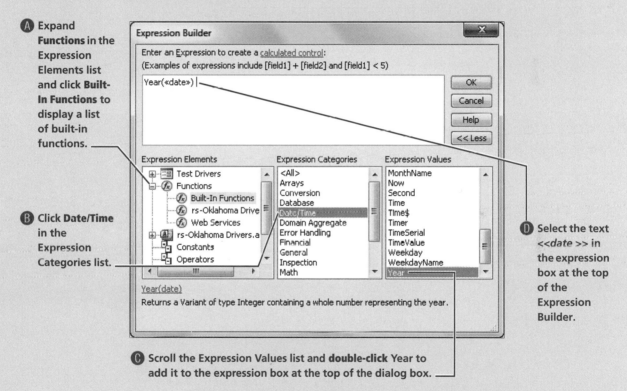

A Expand **Functions** in the Expression Elements list and click **Built-In Functions** to display a list of built-in functions.

B Click **Date/Time** in the Expression Categories list.

D Select the text *<<date >>* in the expression box at the top of the Expression Builder.

C Scroll the Expression Values list and **double-click** Year to add it to the expression box at the top of the dialog box.

5. Follow these steps to complete the expression:

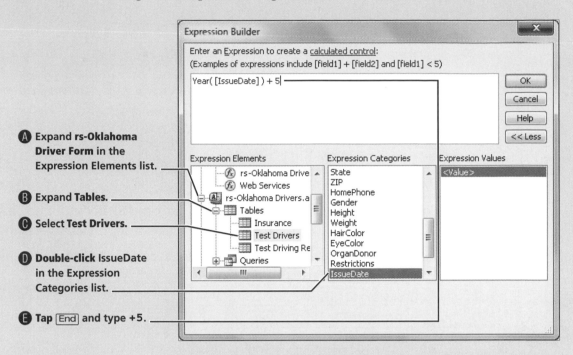

A Expand **rs-Oklahoma Driver Form** in the Expression Elements list.

B Expand **Tables.**

C Select **Test Drivers.**

D Double-click **IssueDate** in the Expression Categories list.

E Tap ⌁End⌁ and type **+5**.

6. Click **OK,** change the Expiration Date label to **Expiration Year**, and switch to **Form View.**

7. Save 🖫 changes to the form and **print** a copy of one record.

8. Close ⊠ the form, **close** the database, and **exit** Access.

Apply Your Skills

Create a Form

The Homestead Properties database currently has two tables—one showing current listings and one showing sold properties. As each new property is listed, new records are added to the Properties table. There are currently no forms for data entry personnel to use to enter new properties. You are assigned the task of creating a form for the company. By building the form from scratch, you can add fields to the form and position them where you want them. In this exercise, you will create a new form and arrange fields on the form.

1. **Open** the as-Homestead Properties database from the Lesson 09 folder and **save** the database as a new file named **as-Homestead Properties Forms**.

2. Open the **Navigation Pane** and select (but do not open) the **Properties** table.

3. Create a new form using **Form Design** and display the **Field List** panel.

4. Drag fields from the **Properties** table **Field List** to appropriate positions on the form and then size, align, and make any necessary adjustments to the controls.

5. Edit and format **control labels** and **text boxes** and set a **background color** for sections of the form.

6. **Save** the form using the form name **Properties**.

7. Display the form in **Form View, print** a copy of one form record, and then **close** the form.

Add a Subform to a Form

The form contained in the Homestead Properties database shows the basic information required for each property. Many clients want to know the price per square foot of the home. Because the value is included in a query, you can add a subform to the main form so that the information is readily available to database users when records in the form are displayed. When you build a form from scratch, Access does not automatically add a subform to the form. In this exercise, you will use tools on the Ribbon to add the subform to the form and modify the control source to identify the data source.

Before You Begin: Your as-Homestead Properties Forms database should be open.

1. Display the Properties form in **Design View.**

2. Locate the **Subform/Subreport** control button on the Ribbon, select it, and then **click** below existing controls in the form to create the control.

3. Use an existing table or query and set the Source Object to **Query: Square Foot Values** and use default setting for remaining query pages.

4. Adjust the size and position of the **subform control** on the form using **Layout View.**

5. **Lock** controls in the subform.

6. View the form in **Form View** and try to edit values in the subform.

7. Switch back to **Design View** and make adjustments to the subform control size, if necessary.

8. **Save** changes to the form and **print** a copy of one record in the form.

9. **Close** the form.

Create a Calculated Control on a Form

When properties are listed with Homestead Properties for more than three months, the price is reduced by 5 percent (.05). In this exercise, you will create two calculated controls on the form: one that calculates the date after which the price is reduced and the other to display the reduced price.

Before You Begin: Your as-Homestead Properties Forms database should be open.

1. Display the Properties form in **Design View** and open the **Property Sheet.**

2. Create a new **text box control** on the form and position it below the **Price** controls.

3. Change the **label text** for the new control to **After**.

4. **Type** the following formula in the appropriate property of the Property Sheet:
   =[DateListed]+90.

5. Create another new **text box control** and place it below the **After** control.

6. Label the new control **Reduced Price:** and **type** a formula in the Property Sheet that tells Access to use the value in the [Price] field and multiply it by 95 percent.

95 percent is the same as .95.

7. Adjust the position of the new field so that the **Reduced Price** controls appear slightly indented below the **After** controls.

8. Format the After controls as **Date** and the new price field controls as bold and currency and then **save** changes to the form.

9. View the form, **print** a copy of record 4, and **close** ✕ the form. **Save** the changes if prompted.

Enhance a Form

The Properties form is almost complete. You can enhance the form by adding a title to the form. In this exercise, you will add control tips to controls on the Properties form and subform. In addition, you will add page number and date controls to the form.

Before You Begin: Your as-Homestead Properties Forms database should be open.

1. Open the **Properties** form in **Design View.**

2. Modify the **form title** to display appropriately on the form in a large decorative font.

3. Add **control tips** to appropriate fields, add the **page number** to the Page Footer section, and add the **date control** to the Form Footer section.

4. **Save** 🖫 changes to the form and **print** a copy of record 10.

5. **Close** ✕ the form, **close** the database, and **exit** Access.

Critical Thinking & Work-Readiness Skills

In the course of working through the following Microsoft Office-based Critical Thinking exercises, you will also be utilizing various work-readiness skills, some of which are listed next to each exercise. Go to labyrinthelab.com/ workreadiness *to learn more about the work-readiness skills.*

9.1 Create, Format, and Enhance a Form

WORK-READINESS SKILLS APPLIED

- Thinking creatively
- Solving problems
- Organizing and maintaining information

iJams has just contracted with Foxy's Gym to serve as a workout facility for iJams personnel. This is increasing Foxy's membership by 30 percent. Foxy's database currently has no forms to use for data entry. You have been contracted by Foxy's manager to create a new form for the database, to format the form, and to add necessary controls to display data appropriately. Use the ct-Foxy's database (Lesson 09 folder) to create a new database named **ct-Foxy's Forms** and create the forms. Review the topics contained in this lesson and be sure to include as many features as are appropriate. Print a copy of one finished form.

9.2 Apply Experience Online

WORK-READINESS SKILLS APPLIED

- Acquiring and evaluating information
- Organizing and maintaining information
- Selecting technology

Many businesses market their services and products on the Internet. Log on to the Internet and locate a website for music production services similar to iJams in your home town or college town. Review features of the site to determine the following:

- The fields for which you can enter values to search for and select listings
- Unique data listed for each business
- The function of each site feature and how it works
- Calculations you can perform using the site
- The date the site was last updated

Create a report in Word named **ct-Music Website Notes** saved to your Lesson 09 folder that identifies features of the site you choose.

9.3 Put Access to Work for Your Business

WORK-READINESS SKILLS APPLIED

- Seeing things in the mind's eye
- Acquiring and evaluating information
- Knowing how to learn

Each field of study has its own unique application for a database. Think about the field of study you are most interested in pursuing and identify an area of the job market in your field that you believe could benefit from using a database. Then, determine what tables/fields would be required for the database. Finally, create a database that contains at least two related tables, input five records of fictitious data in each table, and create a well-designed form that displays a subform with related data. Print copies of each table with the data and a form with data displayed in the main form and subform. Title the database your field of study name and save in your Lesson 09 folder.

Creating Complex Reports

LEARNING OBJECTIVES

After studying this lesson, you will be able to:

■ Import a report into a database

■ Add a subreport to a main report

■ Create a report from a subreport

■ Number items in a report

■ Create calculated controls on a subreport

■ Set page breaks and customize controls

■ Analyze report performance

Database reports summarize data contained in tables or displayed in query results datasheets and enable you to provide meaningful information in a layout that is suitable for printing. Although forms and reports serve two distinctly different purposes within the context of a relational database, the techniques used to customize reports and forms are very similar. By now, you have most likely created reports using both the Report Wizard and Design View and have customized elements of a report. In this lesson, you will import reports from other databases and use additional features to create custom reports.

Billing Customers

iJams, the online music distribution company, is now working with customer orders and wants to devise an invoice report that it can include with customer orders. After reviewing invoices from several different companies, Brett Schneider, fulfillment manager, has sketched out a design for a sample iJams invoice. He is now ready for it to be added to the iJams test database so that he can print a sample copy and circulate it among other administrators in the company. The report he wants created appears similar to the one shown here.

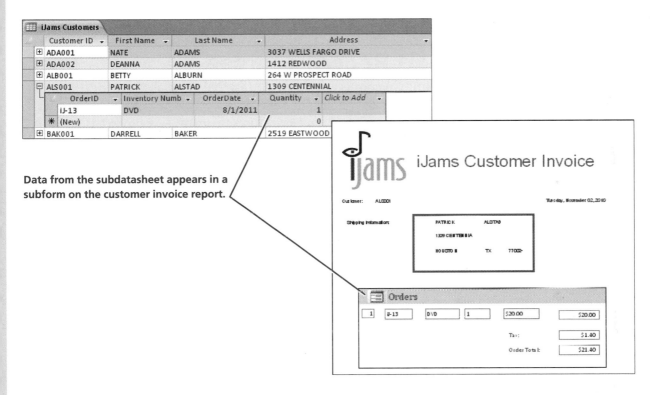

Data from the subdatasheet appears in a subform on the customer invoice report.

10.1 Importing a Report into a Database

Video Lesson labyrinthelab.com/videos

Access offers a variety of ways to create new reports. By now, you have already created a simple report, made reports using the Reports Wizard, and modified the layout of reports using Design View. Another way to get commonly used reports into a database is to import them from another database. Reports such as invoices, sales summaries, and other commonly used business reports normally contain the same basic data—often arranged in the same basic layout. When you locate a report that contains the fields you need, you can import it into an existing database and edit it to create the report you need. Because most companies require some type of invoice to send with customer orders, locating an invoice report that you can import is relatively easy.

Identifying Report Record Sources

Reports that you import retain two connections to their original database: the source database table or query name, which appears in the Record Source property, and field names, which are contained in the source database tables and appear in report control text boxes. As a result, when you import a report from another database, you must break the ties with the source database and establish ties to the new database. You can accomplish this by:

- Editing the Record Source property in the properties box to tie a table or query in the new database to the report.

- Comparing the field names referenced in report control text boxes to those in your database to determine which field names may need to be changed so that Access can locate data to display.

- Editing the field names in the report control text boxes to match those shown in the record source table or query, or renaming fields in the database table to match those shown in the report.

Using SmartTags

Many times, when Access identifies a conflict between an available data or control source and the one identified in the Record Source control, you will see SmartTags onscreen attached to the fields affected. SmartTags appear as small triangles in the upper-left corner of affected controls. You can use the SmartTag to access the Control Source property or the Report Record Source property for the data Access should use for the report control.

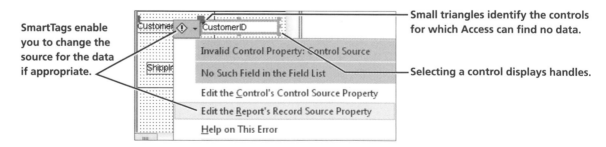

SmartTags enable you to change the source for the data if appropriate.

Small triangles identify the controls for which Access can find no data.

Selecting a control displays handles.

Import a Report and Edit the Record Source

In this exercise, you will import a basic report into a database, rename the report, edit the record source for the report, and view data from a table in your database using the imported report.

1. **Launch** Access, **open** the database named iJams Test in the Lesson 10 folder, and **save** the database as a new database named **iJams Reports**.

2. Choose **External Data→Import→Access** 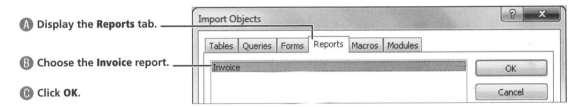 on the Ribbon to open the Get External Data dialog box.

3. Click **Browse**, **open** the Lesson 10 folder, and **double-click** the Invoice database.

4. Choose the Import **Tables, Queries, Forms, Reports, Macros, and Modules into the Current Database** option, and then click **OK**.
   Access opens the Import Objects dialog box and displays object names contained in the Invoice database.

5. Follow these steps to select the Report to import:

A Display the **Reports** tab. ———

B Choose the **Invoice** report. ———

C Click **OK**.

6. Close the **Get External Data** dialog box and open the **Navigation Pane**.

Rename the Report

7. **Right-click** the *Invoice* report name and choose **Rename**.

8. Type **iJams Customer Invoice** and **press** ⏎Enter.
   Access may present a message advising you that the table specified in the report does not exist in this database. You will fix that when you modify the Record Source property.

9. **Right-click** the iJams Customer Invoice report and choose **Design View** to open the report in Design View.

Change the Report Record Source

10. Follow these steps to change the Report Record Source property:

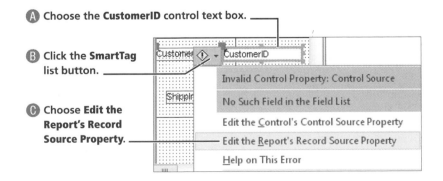

A Choose the **CustomerID** control text box. ———

B Click the **SmartTag** list button. ———

C Choose **Edit the Report's Record Source Property**. ———

Access opens the Property Sheet dialog box.

11. Click the **Record Source** property box and choose **iJams Customers** from the list. *Access clears all conflicts in the reports.*

12. **Save** 🖫 and **close** ✕ the report.

10.2 Adding a Subreport to a Main Report

Video Lesson   labyrinthelab.com/videos

Subreports display subsets of data from related database tables in reports just as subforms do on forms. However, a subreport can display table data by naming a table, query, form, or another report as the source object. Because forms are frequently created before reports, when they already display table data from multiple tables, using the form to create the subreport streamlines report design and often displays data in a better format.

Examining the iJams Database Objects

The invoice report you imported contains only the fields required to report customer information from the iJams Customers table. Invoices normally display the list of items ordered in addition to the customer data. You currently have three tables in the database that contain the data required for the complete invoice—the iJams Customers table, the iJams Inventory table, and the iJams Orders table. Fields from all three tables appear in the iJams Order Processing form—but the fields you want to add to the report appear only in the subform. Using the form, then, makes creating the subreport more efficient.

	iJams Customers	
Customer ID	BLA001	
First Name	CINDY	
Last Name	BLACK	
Address	3910 FRANKLIN AV	
City	HOUSTON	
State	TX	
ZIP	77002	
Phone	(478) 555-1077	

OrderID	Category	Quantity	Sales Price
iJ-4	CD Insert	5	$5.00
iJ-5	Coffee Cup	1	$10.00
iJ-6	MP3 Player	2	$375.00
iJ-1	TV	2	$595.00
＊ (New)			

——This subform contains the data you want to include on the invoice report.

Identifying Procedures for Adding a Subreport

The procedures used to add a subreport to a report are basically the same as those used to add a subform to a form. You can create the report using the Report Wizard or add an unbound subreport control to the report. Then you identify the database object containing the fields you want to display as a subreport.

DEVELOP YOUR SKILLS 10.2.1

Add a Subreport to a Report

In this exercise, you will add a subreport to the iJams Customer Invoice report and identify the iJams Order Subform form as the Source Object for the subreport.

1. Display the iJams Customer Invoice report in **Design View.**

2. Choose **Design→Controls→Subform/Subreport** 📧 on the Ribbon and then click the **Detail** section just below the shipping information control label.
   Access opens the Subreport Wizard.

3. Follow these steps to create the subreport control:

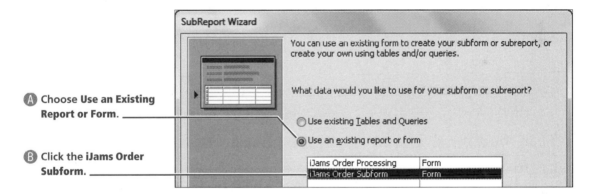

Ⓐ Choose **Use an Existing Report or Form.**

Ⓑ Click the **iJams Order Subform.**

4. Click **Next**, click **Next** again to accept the default links, and then click **Finish.**

5. **Press** F4 to display the Property Sheet and then click the **Data** tab.

6. In the Source Object property box, ensure that **Form.iJams Order Subform** (the top item in the list) is active.

7. Click the **subform label control** for the subreport control and **press** Delete to remove it.

8. Display the report in **Layout View** and adjust the width of each column in the subreport.

9. Drag the **right border** of the subreport to the **6.5"** mark on the horizontal ruler.

10. Choose **Design→Views→View→Print Preview** 🔍 on the Ribbon to switch to Print Preview.

11. Click the **navigation buttons** at the bottom of the window to display several pages of the report, noting pages of the report that contain data in the subreport.

12. **Save** 💾 the changes and **close** ✖ the report.

10.3 Creating a Report from a Subreport

Video Lesson   labyrinthelab.com/videos

The subreport you added to the main report displays table data by using a form as the record source. Changes you make to the layout of the subreport are reflected in the form. To eliminate this problem, you can save the subreport as a separate report in the database, change the Record Source property to the new report object, and then edit the subreport.

As you know, Access allows you to save an existing form as a new form, an existing report as a new report, and so forth. When the form is used as the record source for a subreport, you can display the subreport in a separate window and then save it as a separate report.

QUICK REFERENCE	SAVING A SUBREPORT AS A REPORT
Task	**Procedure**
Open a subreport in a separate window	■ Right-click the subreport on the report in Design View. ■ Choose Subreport in New Window from the shortcut menu.
Save the subreport as a new report	■ Open the subreport in a new window. ■ Choose File→Save Object As to open the Save As dialog box. ■ Type the name of the new report. ■ Select Report from the As list, and then click OK.

DEVELOP YOUR SKILLS 10.3.1
Create a New Report Using a Subreport

In this exercise, you will create and save a new report using the subreport in the iJams Customer Invoice report and edit the source object in the iJams Customer Invoice report to display the new report.

1. Display the iJams Customer Invoice report in **Design View**.

2. **Right-click** the subreport control text box and choose **Subreport in New Window**.
   Access opens the subreport (the iJams Order Subform, in this case) in a separate tabbed window.

 If you do not see the Subreport in New Window command on the shortcut menu, click an area of the main report and then right-click the subreport control again.

3. Choose **File→Save Object As**, and then follow these steps to save the form as a report:

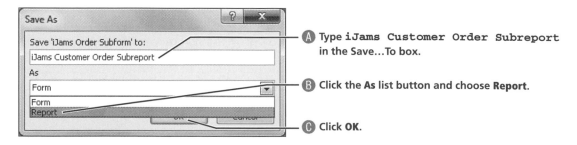

A Type **iJams Customer Order Subreport** in the Save...To box.

B Click the **As** list button and choose **Report**.

C Click **OK**.

4. Add a title containing the word **Orders** to the new report and then **save** the report.

5. **Close** ☒ the new report and then display the iJams Customer Invoice report in **Design View** again.

6. Display the **Property Sheet** and then display the **Data** tab.

7. Select the **subreport control** and change the Source Object property to **Report.iJams Customer Order Subreport**.

8. Switch to **Print Preview** and review the report.

9. **Save** 🖫 and **close** ☒ the report.

10.4 Numbering Items in a Report

Video Lesson labyrinthelab.com/videos

As the number of records contained in a table grows, the length and number of records displayed in a report or subreport also grows. You can number the records in a report to help track items listed. If a report is grouped, you can set the count to restart numbering at the beginning of each group. These numbers serve as an easy reference when you are discussing a report over the telephone or identifying an item in an invoice that you are returning.

Setting Properties to Number Items

By setting the Control Source property for a control, you can add numbering automatically to items in a report. In addition, you can set the Running Sum property to identify the portion of a report for which you want to count items. For example, suppose you have a products report that groups products by category. You can set the Running Sum property to count the items in each group and then start counting again with the next group.

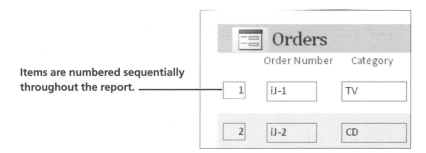

Items are numbered sequentially throughout the report.

Numbering Subreports Separately

A significant limitation to setting a numbering control is that Access does not permit numbering items in a subreport control on a main report. Because you saved the subreport as a separate report, however, you can add the numbering controls directly to the subreport by displaying it in a separate window. Edits you make to the subreport when it is open as a separate item are reflected in the main report the next time you open it.

DEVELOP YOUR SKILLS 10.4.1

Number Items in a Report and Subreport

In this exercise, you will edit the iJams Customer Order Subreport by repositioning controls in the Page Header section and then add an unbound control to the report to count the number of items ordered.

1. Display the iJams Customer Order Subreport in **Design View**.

2. Follow these steps to remove anchor formatting from the Detail Section:

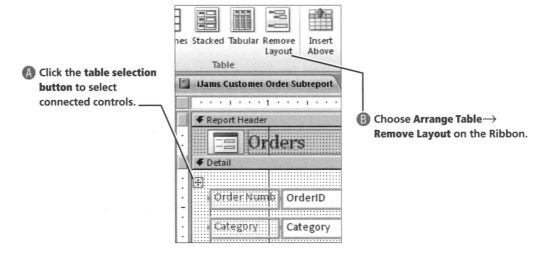

Ⓐ Click the **table selection button** to select connected controls.

Ⓑ Choose **Arrange Table→ Remove Layout** on the Ribbon.

3. **Right-click** the Detail section bar and select **Page Header/Footer** to display the Page Header section of the report.

4. Follow these steps to reposition controls on the subreport:

Ⓐ Move the **control labels** to the Page Header section, size them appropriately, and align them at the top as shown.

Ⓑ Move **control text boxes** in the Detail section, size them appropriately, and align them at the top as shown.

Ⓒ Drag the **Page Footer section** bar up to reduce the size of the Detail section.

5. Choose **Design→Controls→Text Box**  on the Ribbon and then follow these steps to place the control in the Detail section of the report:

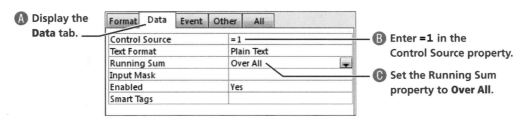

Ⓐ Click to the left of the **OrderID** text box. Notice that the label appears behind the text box control.

Ⓑ Click the **control label** and **delete** it.

Ⓒ Size the control as shown here.

Set Control Properties to Sum

6. Display the **Properties Sheet** panel for the new unbound control.

7. Follow these steps to set the data properties for the control:

Ⓐ Display the **Data** tab.

Ⓑ Enter **=1** in the Control Source property.

Ⓒ Set the Running Sum property to **Over All**.

8. Switch to **Report View** and review the report.
   Access displays the number in the new control and counts 35 records in the report.

9. **Save** 🖫 and **close** ✕ the report.

10. Open the **iJams Customer Invoice** report, display **page 14** of the report, and compare your report to the one shown in the following illustration.

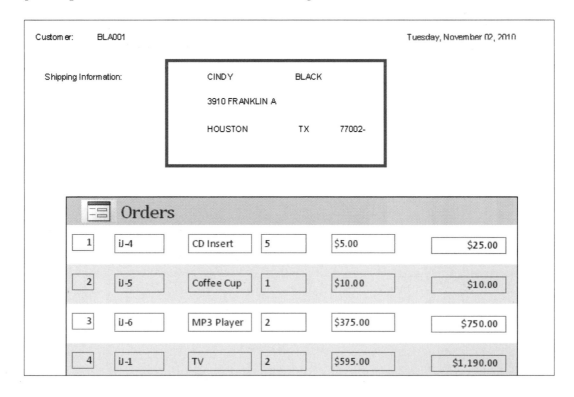

11. **Close** the report.

10.5 Creating Calculated Controls on a Subreport

Video Lesson   labyrinthelab.com/videos

Reports summarize data contained in tables and queries to create valuable information. Calculated fields and controls that appear in queries, on forms, and on reports perform calculations using values from fields contained in tables or displayed on query results datasheets. Adding a calculated field to a report that totals or averages data for a group or subreport often provides valuable information to report reviewers.

Positioning Calculated Controls

Calculated controls are constructed on reports using an unbound control to which you add the formula for the calculation. The position of the calculated control determines how Access performs the calculation.

- When you have a grouped report, add a calculated control to the group footer to sum values for the group and each subordinate subgroup.
- Place a calculated control in a page footer to calculate items on each page.
- Place a calculated control in a report footer to calculate a total for the entire report.

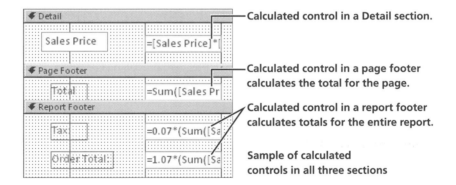

Calculated control in a Detail section.

Calculated control in a page footer calculates the total for the page.

Calculated control in a report footer calculates totals for the entire report.

Sample of calculated controls in all three sections

Create Calculated Controls

In this exercise, you will add three calculated controls to the Report Footer section of the iJams Customer Order Subreport.

1. Display the iJams Customer Order Subreport in **Design View** and display the **Property Sheet All** tab.

2. Follow these steps to create a calculated field in the Detail section:

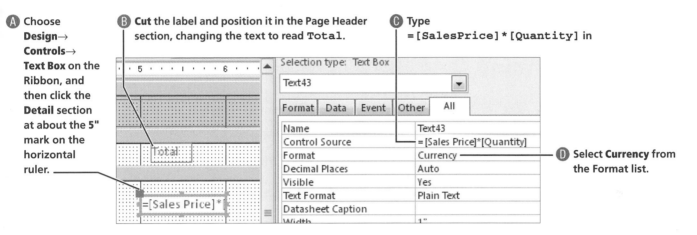

A Choose **Design→ Controls→ Text Box** on the Ribbon, and then click the **Detail** section at about the **5"** mark on the horizontal ruler.

B **Cut** the label and position it in the Page Header section, changing the text to read **Total**.

C **Type** =[SalesPrice]*[Quantity] in

D Select **Currency** from the Format list.

3. Drag the **bottom border** of the Report Footer section down to about the **1"** mark on the vertical ruler to enlarge the Report Footer section.

4. Choose **Design→Controls→Text Box** ![ab] on the Ribbon and click the **Report Footer** section at about the **5"** mark on the horizontal ruler.

5. Display the **Property Sheet** and click the Data tab.

6. Click the **Control Source** property and **type** the following formula into the property box: **=.07*(Sum([Sales Price]*[Quantity]))**.
   This formula tells Access to add (Sum) all the individual item prices and then multiply the total by 7 percent—the sales tax rate.

7. Display the **Property Sheet Format** tab and choose **Currency** as the format.

8. Click the **new control label** and type **Tax:** in the Caption property box.

9. Switch to **Report View** and scroll to the bottom of the report to display the total.
   Access shows the total value of tax is $705.12.

10. Repeat the procedures outlined in **steps 4–9** to:

    ■ Create another **new text box control** below the Tax control.

    ■ **Type** the following formula in the Control Source property box:
      =1.07*(Sum([Sales Price]*[Quantity]))

    This formula tells Access that the total amount of the order is 107 percent (100 percent plus the 7 percent tax) of the total price of all items ordered.

    ■ Format the control as **Currency**.

    ■ **Type** the following control label in the Caption property box: **Order Total**.

11. **Preview** the last page of the report and compare the last few lines of your report to the one shown in the following illustration.

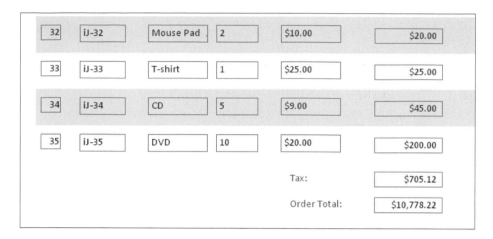

32	iJ-32	Mouse Pad	2	$10.00	$20.00
33	iJ-33	T-shirt	1	$25.00	$25.00
34	iJ-34	CD	5	$9.00	$45.00
35	iJ-35	DVD	10	$20.00	$200.00
				Tax:	$705.12
				Order Total:	$10,778.22

12. **Close** ☒ the subreport, **saving** changes when prompted.

Growing a Subreport

Video Lesson labyrinthelab.com/videos

When the number of records or amount of data displayed in a subreport varies, as it does for customer invoices, you can set the Can Grow property setting to allow the space allotted to the subreport on a main report to expand so that more data appears vertically in the subreport. You can also change the orientation of the print layout to allow more horizontal space on each report page.

QUICK REFERENCE	SETTING MARGINS, ORIENTATION, CAN GROW, AND CAN SHRINK PROPERTIES
Task	**Procedure**
Set report margins	■ From Design or Layout View, choose Page Layout→Page Size→Margins on the Ribbon. ■ Choose the margin form to apply. *or* ■ From Print Preview, choose Print Preview→Page Size→Margins on the Ribbon. ■ Choose the margin form to apply.
Set orientation	■ From Design or Layout View, choose Page Layout→Page Layout on the Ribbon. ■ Choose the Portrait or Landscape orientation to apply. *or* ■ From Print Preview, choose Print Preview→Page Layout on the Ribbon. ■ Choose the Portrait or Landscape orientation to apply.
Set Can Grow property	■ Display the Property Sheet and click the Format tab. ■ Click the subreport control. ■ Set the Can Grow property to Yes.
Set Can Shrink property	■ Display the Property Sheet and click the Format tab. ■ Click the subreport control. ■ Set the Can Shrink property to Yes.

Set the Can Grow Property and Report Layout

In this exercise, you will adjust the layout and margins of the main iJams Customer Invoice report and set the Can Grow property.

Before You Begin: Your iJams Reports database should be open.

1. Open the iJams Customer Invoice report in **Design View** and display **page 4**.

2. Change the following settings:
    - Choose **Page Setup→Page Layout→Landscape** [A] on the Ribbon.
    - Choose **Page Setup→Page Size→Margins** [ ] on the Ribbon and choose Narrow.

3. **Save** [ ] changes to the report.

4. Display the **Property Sheet** and then display the **Format** tab.

5. Click the **subreport control** and set the following properties:
    - Set the Can Grow property to **Yes** if it is set differently.
    - Set the Can Shrink property to **Yes**.

6. Adjust the **horizontal width** of the subreport control to display all data.

7. **Save** [ ] changes and display **page 4** of the report in **Print Preview**.
    Notice the enlarged subreport area in the following illustration. Now the tax and total calculations appear.

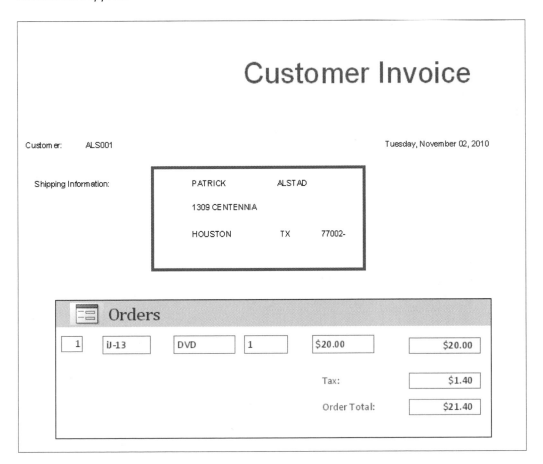

10.6 Setting Page Breaks and Customizing Controls

Video Lesson   labyrinthelab.com/videos

As you reviewed pages of the iJams Customer Invoice report in Report View, you most likely noticed that the number of records displayed on each page varied, depending on whether or not data appeared in the subreport as well as on the number of items the customer ordered. By default, when you view the report in Print Preview, data for each customer/record automatically appears on a separate page even though multiple records appear when the report is displayed in Report View.

When you import a report from another source, you frequently need to customize the report so that it meets the needs of the new database. Many businesses customize reports to display a company name and logo, for instance. Depending on the information you are reporting, it may also be necessary to adjust the page layout or change the margins or orientation, as you did in the last exercise, so that the report fits more attractively on a page. It is also sometimes wise to add a page break control to ensure that the invoice for each customer starts on a new page.

Positioning the Page Break Control

When each page of a report such as an invoice is to be sent to different people, it is also important that each invoice in the report prints on a separate sheet of paper. You can set page breaks to ensure that each customer invoice prints on a separate page. It is important to position the page break at the end of the detail section so that Access knows to start a new page before printing the next page header.

QUICK REFERENCE	ADDING PAGE BREAK CONTROLS
Task	**Procedure**
Add a page break control	■ Choose Design→Controls→Insert Page Break on the Ribbon. ■ Drag the Page Footer section bar down to provide space at the bottom of the Detail section. ■ Click the Detail section at the position on the Detail section where you want the page to break.

Add Logo, Title, Date, and Page Break Controls to a Report

In this exercise, you will "clean up" the iJams Customer Invoice report by customizing the imported report. You will edit control text to add iJams to the title, insert a picture of a logo, and set page breaks to print each invoice on a separate page.

Before You Begin: Your iJams Reports database should be open.

1. Display the iJams Customer Invoice report in **Design View**.

2. Click the **Customer Invoice** title control in the Page Header section, and then follow these steps to edit the Title:

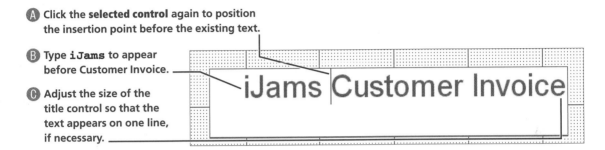

A Click the **selected control** again to position the insertion point before the existing text.

B Type **iJams** to appear before Customer Invoice.

C Adjust the size of the title control so that the text appears on one line, if necessary.

Add a Logo to the Page Header

3. Choose **Design→Header/Footer→Logo** 🖼 on the Ribbon and **double-click** the iJams.bmp file in the Lesson 10 folder.
   Access adds the logo to the Report Header section. You want the logo to appear on each report page, so you need to move it.

4. Drag the logo to the **Page Header** section and position it on the left side of the title.

5. Size the control to enlarge it and then set the Size Mode property for the control to **Stretch**.

Add a Date Control to the Report

Now you will remove the existing Order Date field control and replace it with a Date control.

6. Delete the **Order Date** label control from the Detail section.

7. Choose **Design→Header/Footer→Date & Time** 📅 on the Ribbon to add just the Date (not the time) to the Report Header section.

8. **Cut** the control from the Report Header section and **paste** it into the Detail section, positioning it at the right side of the report even with the Customer ID control.

Add a Page Break Control

9. Follow these steps to position the page break:

A Drag the **Page Footer** section bar down to provide space at the bottom of the Detail section.

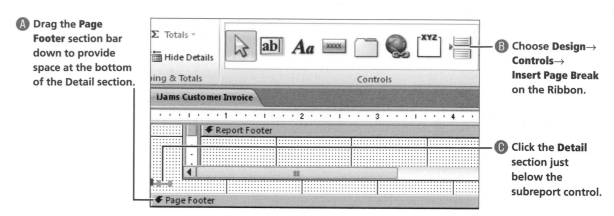

B Choose **Design→ Controls→ Insert Page Break** on the Ribbon.

C Click the **Detail** section just below the subreport control.

10. **Preview** the report and navigate to additional report pages.
For this report, the page break causes an extra page to appear for each record. As a result, you should delete the page break control.

11. Display **Design View**, select the **Page Break** control, and **press** [Delete] to remove it.

12. **Save** 🖫 and **close** ✕ the report.

10.7 Analyzing Report Performance

Video Lesson   labyrinthelab.com/videos

Access tracks each database object and identifies how tables, queries, forms, and reports are related. In addition, Access tracks how you use each object within the database. The changes you have made to the database by importing a report, editing the report structure, creating a subreport based on a form, saving the form as a report, and then changing the record source for the subreport are a bit more complex than creating a simple report and adding a subreport that is based on another table or query. You have also made other changes since you last checked the performance of the database.

What the Performance Analyzer Analyzes

To ensure that all objects in a database work together in an efficient manner, you can run the *Performance Analyzer*. The Performance Analyzer:

■ Analyzes database performance by reviewing each database object, identifying potential errors, and recommending modifications to objects and fields within each object to maintain optimum efficiency in the database

■ Compares relationships between database tables and identifies data redundancy

- Identifies items such as mismatched field definitions and displays a list of these instances so that you can consider editing object definitions
- Locates errors that could result in inaccurate data analysis and any disconnects between forms/subforms and reports/subreports
- Identifies fields and property settings that can slow down the running of filters and queries as well as the generation of reports

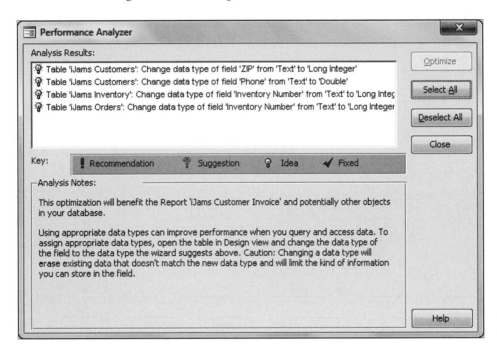

A sample Performance Analyzer report

You can use the Performance Analyzer to analyze all objects in a database or selected objects. You can even change settings to instruct the analyzer to make the necessary corrections for you.

DEVELOP YOUR SKILLS 10.7.1
Analyze Report Performance

In this exercise, you will run the Performance Analyzer on the iJams Customer Invoice report and review suggested performance analysis.

Before You Begin: Your iJams Reports database should be open.

1. Click (but do not open) the **iJams Customer Invoice** report in the Navigation Pane.

2. Choose **Database Tools→Analyze→Analyze Performance** on the Ribbon to start the Performance Analyzer.
   Because you selected the report before starting the performance analyzer, Access displays the active object page in the Performance Analyzer window.

3. Click **Select All** to select all reports, and then click **OK**.

Access analyzes the reports in the database and presents the following report.

All these ideas affect fields containing numbers that will not be used in calculations. Therefore, it's OK for them to be text data types.

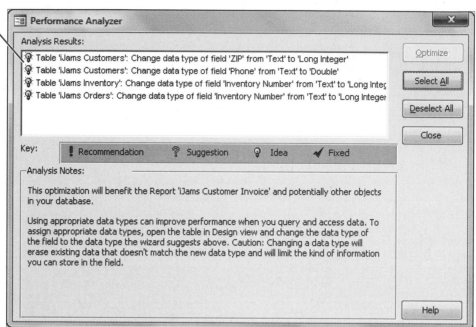

4. **Close** the dialog box, **close** the database, and **exit** Access.

10.8 Concepts Review

Concepts Review   labyrinthelab.com/acc10

To check your knowledge of the key concepts introduced in this lesson, complete the Concepts Review quiz by going to the URL listed above. If your classroom is using Labyrinth eLab, you may complete the Concepts Review quiz from within your eLab course.

Reinforce Your Skills

Import a Report and Edit a Record Source

The state licensing bureau is continuing its work to develop a database that they plan to implement and then market to states so that each state can maintain accurate records for licensed drivers. One of the database developers identified a report layout from a database submitted as an example by the state of Louisiana. The report is similar to the one they want to include in their database. In this exercise, you will import the report and then customize it to meet the needs of the national database.

1. **Launch** Access, **open** the rs-Oklahoma Drivers database from the Lesson 10 folder, and create a **new** database named **rs-Driver Reports**.

2. Choose **External Data→Import & Link→Access** ![icon] on the Ribbon to open the Get External Data dialog box.

3. Click the **Browse** button, locate, and **double-click** the rs-Sample Driver Report database in the Lesson 10 folder.

4. Choose the **Import Tables, Queries, Forms, Reports, Macros, and Modules Into the Current Database** option and click **OK**.

5. Click the **Reports** tab, click the **Sample Drivers Report** report, and then click **OK** to import the report.

6. Close the **Get External Data** dialog box and display the new report in **Design View**.

Edit the Record Source

Notice the triangles in the upper-left corner of each control in the Detail section that identify errors finding the data. You need to change the record source to correct this.

7. **Press** F4 to open the Property Sheet and click the Data tab.

8. Click the **Record Source** property and select **Oklahoma Drivers** from the Record Source list.

9. Switch to **Report View** and review the report data.

10. **Save** ![save icon] and **close** ![close icon] the report.

Add Fields to a Report and Arrange Report Controls

The sample drivers report is designed to list some driver data in a tabular layout. To prepare the layout of the report to accommodate the subreport, you need to rearrange the controls on the report. In this exercise, you will add fields to a report, change the layout of the report, and arrange controls. Feel free to use your own report design.

Before You Begin: Your rs-Driver Reports database should be open.

1. Display the Sample Drivers Report in **Design View**.

2. Drag the top of the **Page Footer** section bar down to expand the Detail section.

Arrange Controls

3. Drag controls in the **Detail** section to appear as shown in the following illustration.

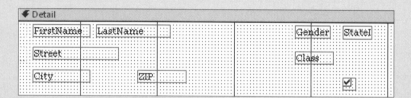

4. Follow these steps to select multiple controls and change the font color:

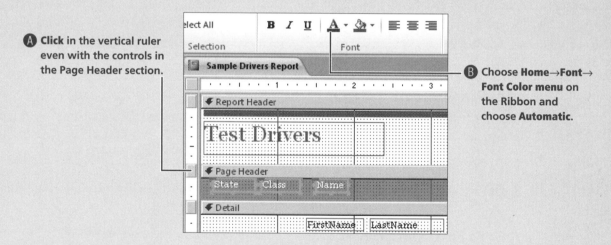

Ⓐ **Click** in the vertical ruler even with the controls in the Page Header section.

Ⓑ Choose **Home→Font→ Font Color menu** on the Ribbon and choose **Automatic**.

5. **Click** a blank area of the report to deselect all controls.

6. **Drag** each of the following control labels from the Page Header section to the Detail section, positioning them beside the corresponding control text box: Gender, Donor, Class, Name, and Street.

7. Repeat the procedures outlined in **step 4** to select all remaining controls in the Page Header section and then **press** ⌷Delete⌷ to remove them.

Format and Edit Controls

8. Select the **State** text box control in the Detail section and then format the control using these guidelines:

   ■ Set the font size to **48**.

   ■ Size the State control to show **Sta** in the control box.

   ■ Change to a font **other than** Georgia.

   ■ Set the font color to a shade of **maroon**.

9. Change the name of the Street label to **Address**.

10. Choose **Design→Tools→Add Existing Fields** ▦ on the Ribbon to open the Field List.

Add Controls

11. **Drag** the following fields from the field list and position them along the bottom of the Detail section: Height, Weight, HairColor, EyeColor.

Arrange and Edit the Title

12. **Drag** the Test Drivers control from the Report Header section to the Page Header section and then **double-click** the word Test and type **Oklahoma**.

13. **Save** 🖫 changes to the report and then display the report in **Report View** to preview it.

14. **Print** a copy of one report page and then **close** ☒ the report.

REINFORCE YOUR SKILLS 10.3

Add a Subreport to a Report

Insurance information on file for each driver is an important part of a driver's record and should be included for each driver in the report. In this exercise, you will add the insurance data to the Sample Drivers Reports report.

Before You Begin: Your rs-Driver Reports database should be open.

1. Display the Sample Drivers Reports report in **Design View**.

2. Drag the **Page Footer** section bar down to make room for the subreport control.

3. Choose **Design→Controls→Subform/Subreport** ▦ on the Ribbon and click the **Detail** section of the report just below the Height control label.

4. Choose **Cancel** to close the wizard and then **press** F4 to open the Property Sheet.

5. Click the **Source Object** property and choose **Form.Insurance** from the source object list.

6. **Drag** the right side of the report to about the **9"** mark on the horizontal ruler.

7. Display **Layout View** and choose **Page Setup→Page Layout→Landscape** to change the layout of the report.

8. Adjust the size of the **subreport control** to display all columns and delete the **subreport control label**.

9. **Save** 🖫 changes to the report, **print** a copy of page 1, and then **close** the report.

Save a Subreport as a New Report and Adjust Margins

The subreport you added to the report using a form can be saved as a stand-alone report so that changes made to the form cause no problems with the report. In this exercise, you will save the subreport as a separate report and adjust the margins so that the control fits on the report page.

Before You Begin: *Your rs-Driver Reports database should be open.*

1. Display the Sample Drivers Report in **Design View**.

2. **Right-click** the subreport control and select **Subreport in New Window** on the shortcut menu.

3. Choose **File→Save Object As** to open the Save As dialog box.

4. Type **Insurance Proof Subreport** in the Save Form To box.

5. Choose **Report** from the As drop-down list and click **OK**.

6. **Close** ☒ all objects and then display the Sample Drivers report in **Design View**.

7. Display the **Property Sheet**.

8. Click the **Source Object** property and choose **Report.Insurance Proof Subreport** from the property list.

9. Close the **Property Sheet** and then size the subreport control to fit the size of the subreport page displayed.

10. **Drag** the right page edge of the report back to the **9"** mark on the horizontal ruler.

11. Choose **Page Setup→Page Size→Margins** ▦ on the Ribbon and then choose **Narrow**.

12. **Save** 🖫 changes to the report, **preview** it and compare your report to the one shown, and then **close** the report.

Oklahoma Drivers

Name	John COOK	Gender	F
Address	7015 Westchester Dri	Class	Adult
	Omega 73764	Donor	☑

OK

Height: 5'7"   Weight: 135   HairColor: Blonde   EyeColor: Brown

Insurance

DriverID	123456789	Agency State	
Auto Insurance	All State	Agency ZIP	
Agent ID	AS2234	Agency Phone	(703) 555-6657
Agent First Name		AutoType	Toyota

REINFORCE YOUR SKILLS 10.5

Edit a Subreport and Number Records

The field arrangement on the subreport displays multiple records that are difficult to discern. In addition, some drivers have multiple cars for which they have registered insurance. It would be helpful to number the insurance listings. In this exercise, you will modify the subreport and add a number control to the subreport.

Before You Begin: *Your rs-Driver Reports database should be open.*

1. Display the Insurance Proof Subreport in **Design View.**

2. Choose **Design→Controls→Text Box** 📦 on the Ribbon and click the report **Detail** section just below the Agent Last Name label.

3. Delete the new **Unbound** control label and **press** F4 to display the Property Sheet.

4. Format the **new control** by sizing it similarly to the State field on the main form. *The State field on the main form was formatted using 48 point font size, maroon font color, and a font type other than Georgia.*

5. Type **=1** in the Control Source property and set the Running Sum property to **Over All.**

6. Close the **Property Sheet** and adjust the size and position of controls on the subreport to display all values and label text.

7. **Save** 💾 changes to the subreport, and then **preview** it.

8. **Close** ☒ the subreport and **open** the Sample Drivers Report.

9. Review pages of the report, and then switch back to **Design View** to make necessary adjustments to control and report size.

10. **Save** 💾 changes to the report and print a copy of **page 7.**

11. **Close** ☒ the report.

Insert Page Breaks and Analyze Reports

You have added a variety of different objects to the sb-Driver Reports database. Before continuing with additional projects, it would be a good idea to analyze the performance of database objects. In this exercise, you will insert page breaks in the report design and then analyze the performance of reports in the database.

Before You Begin: Your rs-Driver Reports database should be open.

1. Display the Sample Drivers Reports report in **Design View**.

2. Choose **Design→Controls→Insert Page Break** on the Ribbon and click the **Detail** section of the report just below the subreport control on the left side of the report.

3. Switch to **Print Preview** and navigate each report page.

4. **Save** and **close** the report.

5. Select the **Sample Drivers Report** in the Reports list, but do not open it.

6. Choose **Database Tools→Analyze→Analyze Performance** on the Ribbon to open the Performance Analyzer dialog box.

7. Check both the **Sample Drivers Report** and **Insurance Proof Subreport** checkboxes in the Reports list.

8. Click **OK**.
   Access displays a list of three ideas—all related to changing the Text data types for fields containing numeric data to Number data types.

9. **Close** the dialog box and choose **Database Tools→Analyze→Analyze Performance** on the Ribbon to open the Performance Analyzer dialog box again.

10. Click the **All Object Types** tab, click the **Select All** button to select all objects, and then click **OK** to run the Analyzer.

11. Review ideas presented, **close** the dialog box, **and** close the database.

Apply Your Skills

APPLY YOUR SKILLS 10.1

Create a Report from a Form

The Homestead Properties database currently has three tables—one showing current listings, one showing property details for listings, and one showing sold properties. When clients who want to buy properties come into the office, office personnel want to be able to print a report that shows not only the property data—location, cost, and so forth—but would also like to show data from the property details table. Because the main part of the report you want to build exists in a form, you can use the form to create the report. In this exercise, you will create the main report using an existing form.

1. **Open** the as-Homestead Properties database contained in the Lesson 10 folder and **save** it as a new file named **as-Homestead Reports**.

2. Open the **Properties** form and review the form details.

3. **Save** the form as a report named **Active Listings**. **Open** the report.

4. Display the report in **Print Preview** and navigate pages of the report.

5. **Save** 💾 the report, **print** a copy of page 1, and then **close** ✕ the report.

APPLY YOUR SKILLS 10.2

Add a Subreport and Page Break to a Report

The Active Listings report contained in the as-Homestead Reports database shows the basic information required for each property. It does not, however, show the details about the home that appear in the Property Details table. In this exercise, you will add the details data as a subreport on the main report and add a sort order so that records display by listing number.

Before You Begin: Your as-Homestead Reports database should be open.

1. Display the Active Listings report in **Design View**.

2. Add a **subreport** to the Detail section of the report, placing it just below the existing report data.

3. Set the Source Object property to show the **Property Details** table data and delete the **control label**.

4. Choose **Design→Grouping & Totals→Group & Sort** 🔲 to open the Group, Sort, and Total panel.

5. Click the **Add a Sort** button in the Group, Sort, and Total panel and select **Listing#** as the field to sort on.

6. Switch to **Layout View** and size columns in the subreport to fit the data contained in the columns.

7. **Size** the subreport control to display all seven columns and **save** 💾 changes to the report.

8. Preview the report, switch back to **Design View**, and make any necessary adjustments to the size and position of the subreport control.

9. Add a **page break** below the subreport.

10. Display the **Page Header/Footer** for the report and move the title from the Report Header section to the Page Header section.

11. Hide the **Report Header** section and **save** 💾 changes to the report.

12. **Print** a copy of one page of the report and then **close** ☒ it.

Create a Simple Report and Number Items

Homestead Properties likes to maintain a running count of sold properties that they print and distribute to all realtors each week. They would like to create a report that they can use to generate the report each week. In this exercise, you will create a new simple report and add a numbering control to the report.

Before You Begin: Your as-Homestead Reports database should be open.

1. Create a new **Simple Report** based on the Sold Properties table and review the report.

2. **Save** the report as **Sold Homestead Properties**.

3. Display the new report in **Design View** and remove automatic layout ties from all controls in each report section.

4. Change the margins to **Narrow** and adjust the position and size of the controls to fit the data and label text using **Layout View**.

5. Delete the **Sold** controls, format the **Price** control text box to show currency, and add an appropriate **title** to the report.

6. Increase the **size** of the Page Header section and move the **title** to the Page Header section.

7. Hide the **Report Header/Footer** sections. Choose **Yes** if warned that hiding the sections will remove controls from the sections.

8. Add an **unbound control** to the Detail section of the report, delete the **control label**, and set the **control properties** to number items over the complete report.

9. Set the orientation of the report to **Landscape** and drag the right edge of the report page to about the **10"** mark on the horizontal ruler.

10. **Save** 💾 the report as **Sold Homestead Properties**, **preview** the report, and **print** a copy of the last page of the report.

11. **Close** ☒ the report.

Create a Calculated Control and Analyze the Database

As realtors review the Sold Properties report, they would like to know the total value of real estate sold. Each property listed by the company nets 3 percent of the sales price. Because all properties on the sold list were listed by agents from Homestead Properties, they would also like to see the value of their portion of the sales price. In this exercise, you will create calculated controls to show the commission earned by the company for each property and a total amount earned for all sold properties. You will also analyze the database.

Before You Begin: Your as-Homestead Reports database should be open.

1. Display the Sold Homestead Properties report in **Design View**.

2. Create a **new unbound control** and position it at the right side of the Detail section of the report.

3. Set the formula in the Control Source property: **=.03*[Price]**.

4. Add a label containing the text **Listing Profits** to the Page Header section for the new calculated control.

5. Display the **Report Footer** section and create an **unbound control** in the Report Footer section below the Price column, label the control **Total Sales**, and add the formula **=Sum([Price])**.

6. Format both controls to display the values as **currency**.

7. Use the **Format Painter** to copy the format from one standard column heading to the labels of both new controls, if necessary to make them uniform in appearance.

8. **Preview** the report and **print** a copy of the last report page.

9. **Save** 💾 changes to the report and run the **Performance Analyzer** to analyze all database reports.

10. **Close** ✕ the report, and then **close** the database.

Critical Thinking & Work-Readiness Skills

In the course of working through the following Microsoft Office-based Critical Thinking exercises, you will also be utilizing various work-readiness skills, some of which are listed next to each exercise. Go to labyrinthelab.com/workreadiness *to learn more about the work-readiness skills.*

10.1 Create, Format, and Enhance a Report

WORK-READINESS SKILLS APPLIED

- Solving problems
- Serving clients/customers
- Improving or designing systems

Foxy's gym, the exercise facility for iJams personnel, has contracted you to create a report to distribute with employee paychecks that shows employee data and hours worked. A sample of the report administrators want was located in the ct-Easy Up Sports database (Lesson 10 folder) that Foxy's recently acquired. Your task is to import that report and use it to create the new report. Use the ct-Foxy's database (Lesson 10 folder) to create a new database named **ct-Foxy's Reports**. Import the ct-Easy Up Sports database Personnel report to create the new report named **Foxy's Paystub**. Formulas required for calculated fields appear in a tabbed page on the report you import and can be removed from the report after you add the fields to the new report. Save and print a copy of page 5 of the report.

10.2 Add a Logo and Analyze Reports

WORK-READINESS SKILLS APPLIED

- Acquiring and evaluating information
- Interpreting and communication information
- Solving problems

Foxy's gym wants to add the logo to each database object so people begin to associate exercise and health with Foxy's. Add the Foxy's Logo (Lesson 10 folder) to the Foxy's Paystub report you created in the previous exercise. When both reports are complete, run an analysis on the reports to determine ways to optimize performance.

How many suggestions does Access make? Why? How many critical errors does Access find? How can you correct them? Record your answers in a Word document named **ct-Questions** saved to your Lesson 10 folder.

10.3 Train On Reports

WORK-READINESS SKILLS APPLIED

- Knowing how to learn
- Acquiring and evaluating information
- Reading

Though this class, with its textbook and associated materials, may be the best way initially to learn Access skills for most learners, the Microsoft website is a great source for learning as well.

Explore the available online training sessions for reports. Review at least two sessions to learn more about grouped reports and report summarization. Identify at least two report features that you want to learn more about. Experiment with the two features using the ct-Foxy's Reports database you created in Critical Thinking 10.1.

Create a Word document named **ct-Online Learning** in your Lesson 10 folder that identifies the features that you have learned more about and how or why these features are important to you. Print the report.

Customizing the Database Interface and Setting Security

LEARNING OBJECTIVES

After studying this lesson, you will be able to:

- Set Access options
- Split a database
- Set a database password
- Create a database switchboard
- Create a Navigation Form
- Set and modify startup options
- Encrypt a database with a password

Now that you have learned how to create, modify, and customize tables, forms, and reports, you can begin to focus on sharing the database with other users. Designing a user interface makes the database easy for novice users to enter and process data. As you may imagine, sharing databases comes with the risk of data corruption and loss. It is important to protect a database from data loss and unauthorized access and editing. In this lesson, you will customize Access 2010 settings, explore database security features, and set a database password. You will also create two user interfaces: a Switchboard and a Navigation Form. Finally, you will split a database so database tables and their data are protected, but individuals who use the database can create and modify their own personal queries, forms, and reports.

Customizing – As You Like It

The prototype of the database being designed for iJams is almost complete. After reviewing the database, Carthic Maddix, iJams' owner, is pleased with the designs of the forms and reports. He is, however, a bit concerned about the ease with which those who will be maintaining the data in the database will find the database. In addition, he is concerned about the security of the database and the data it contains. Finally, he is concerned that the display of the database objects will be different for each individual who uses the database and would like to see Access settings customized. He wants to customize the settings for the database so that it appears the same regardless of who uses the database, to create a user interface that makes it easier to use, and to secure the database for all users.

A Switchboard form contains buttons for performing common tasks.

A Navigation Form displays tabs at the top and along the side of the form to access groups of objects and display them in the same work area, one item at a time.

11.1 Setting Access Options

Video Lesson   labyrinthelab.com/videos

As you may have discovered in other Microsoft Office applications such as Word and Excel, you can set options to control the way the application performs. The same is true in Access 2010. Features in Access Options enable users to change settings that control the color of their datasheets, set default fonts, create sections on the Navigation Pane, add a title to the application window, customize the quick access toolbar, and set a default start form such as a switchboard, to name a few of the most popular options. Some options control the settings for the active database while other options control the settings for all databases used on a particular machine.

The pages of the Access Options dialog box contain far too many features to cover completely. Never hesitate to explore these settings and options on your own.

Displaying Access Options

The Access Options dialog box groups features according to type and lists the option categories in a panel on the left side of the dialog box. Selecting another category in the panel changes the displayed options in the panel on the right side of the dialog box. As you review different option groups, you will discover that some options are used frequently while others are rarely used.

Option
categories

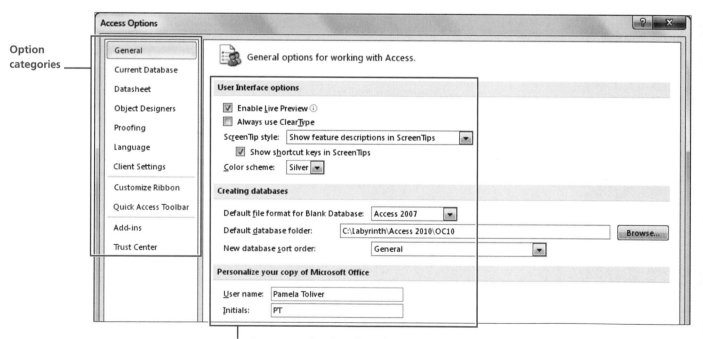

Option groups for the selected General category show the current settings.

Display and Navigate Access Options

In this exercise, you will display the Access Options dialog box.

1. **Launch** Access, **open** the iJams database from the Lesson 11 folder, and **enable content**, if prompted.

2. **Save** the database as a new database named **iJams Custom**.

3. Choose **File→Options** to open the Access Options dialog box.

4. Follow these steps to navigate the Access Options dialog box:

Ⓐ Choose the **Current Database** category and review the options.

Ⓑ Choose each additional category, review options available in each category, and then choose the **Object Designers** category.

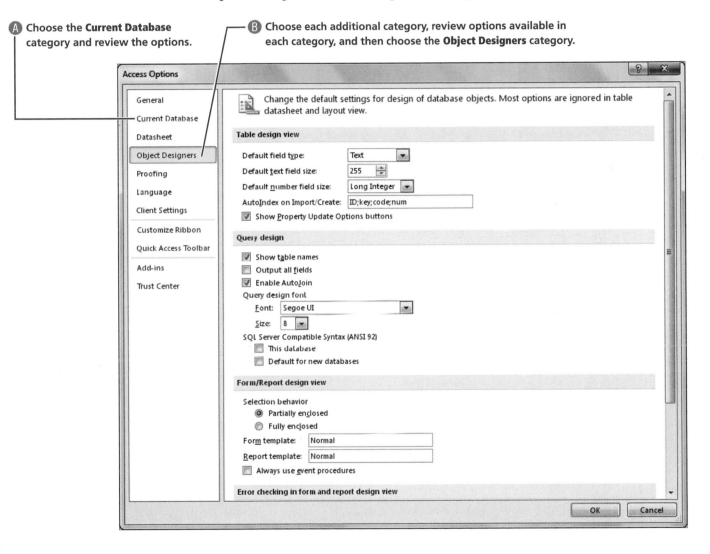

5. Click **OK** to close the dialog box without changing any options.

Enabling Error Checking

Video Lesson labyrinthelab.com/videos

Error-checking features in Access 2010 enable you to detect errors as you create and customize database objects. As a result, Error Checking options appear in the Object Designers category of Access Options. You can enable or disable each of the following error-checking items:

- Enable error checking
- Check for unassociated label and control
- Check for new unassociated labels
- Check for keyboard shortcut errors

- Check for invalid control properties
- Check for common report errors
- Change the color Access applies to indicate errors

 Changing the Error Checking options affects *all* databases used on the computer.

Customizing the Navigation Pane

The Navigation Pane is your tool for selecting database objects, identifying objects associated with each object type, and switching among database objects. You have also used the Navigation Pane to display objects in different views. As a result, you most likely have discovered its usefulness. You can customize the Navigation Pane to contain additional sections to make the pane even more useful.

Identifying Navigation Pane Categories and Groups

The Navigation Options dialog box shows two list boxes: one that identifies the categories of objects displayed on the Navigation Pane and one that shows the groups available for display on the Pane.

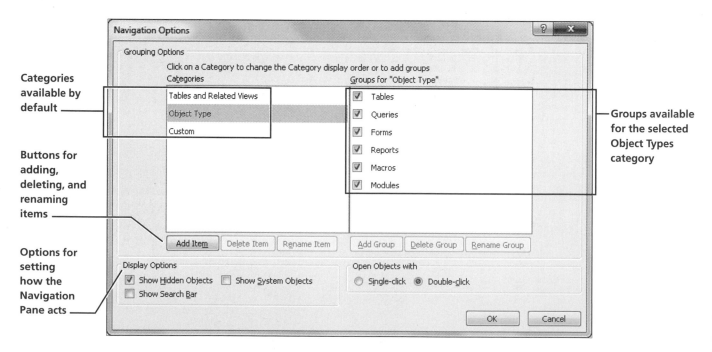

Working with Groups

Groups for the Object Types and Tables and Related Views categories are set and Access prevents you from changing, deleting, or adding additional object type groups to these categories. The Custom category, on the other hand, is fully customizable and allows you to rename, delete, and add groups to the category. When you add or rename groups on the Navigation Pane, you must then reassign objects to the groups so that Access knows where to place them.

Customizing the Navigation Pane controls the settings for the active database only. As a result, you would have to repeat this procedure to customize the Navigation Pane for other databases.

DEVELOP YOUR SKILLS 11.1.2
Set Error Checking and Customize the Navigation Pane

In this exercise, you will display the Access Options dialog box, set error-checking options, customize the Navigation Pane, and assign objects to new Navigation Pane groups.

1. Choose **File→Options**, and then follow these steps to set Error Checking options:

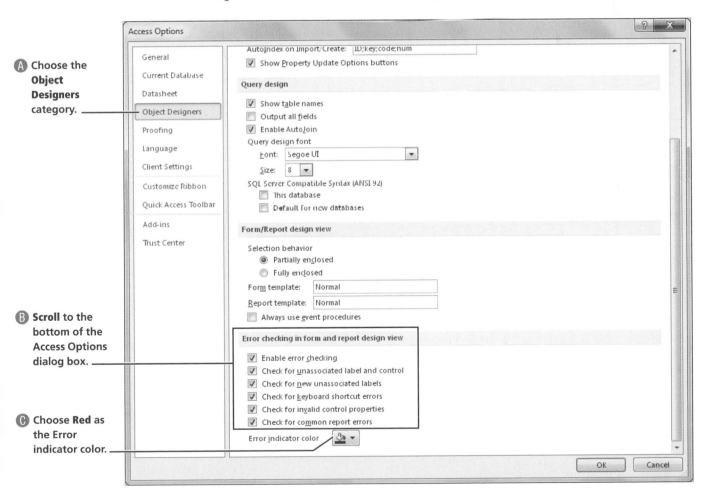

A Choose the **Object Designers** category.

B **Scroll** to the bottom of the Access Options dialog box.

C Choose **Red** as the Error indicator color.

2. Follow these steps to customize the Navigation Pane:

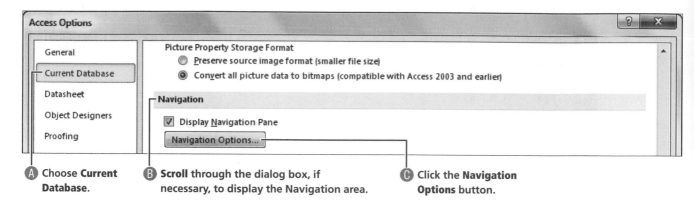

Ⓐ Choose **Current Database**.

Ⓑ **Scroll** through the dialog box, if necessary, to display the Navigation area.

Ⓒ Click the **Navigation Options** button.

Access displays the Navigation Options dialog box.

3. Choose **Custom**, and then follow these steps to rename a Navigation Pane category:

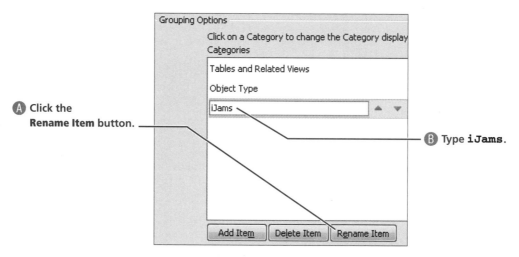

Ⓐ Click the **Rename Item** button.

Ⓑ Type **iJams**.

4. Follow these steps to rename and add Navigation Pane groups:

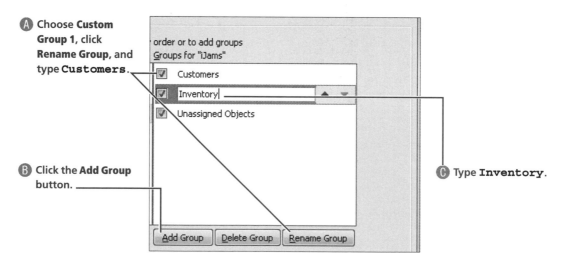

Ⓐ Choose **Custom Group 1**, click **Rename Group**, and type **Customers**.

Ⓑ Click the **Add Group** button.

Ⓒ Type **Inventory**.

5. Click **OK** to close the Navigation Options dialog box and then click **OK** to close the Access Options dialog box.

6. Follow these steps to display the new iJams category:

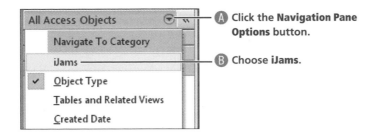

A Click the **Navigation Pane Options** button.

B Choose **iJams**.

Access places all objects for the iJams category into the Unassigned Objects group.

7. Expand the **Unassigned Objects** group on the Navigation Pane, **right-click** the iJams Customers table object, and choose **Add to Group→Customers**.

8. Repeat the procedures outlined in **step 7** to assign the following objects to the group identified:

Object	Group
iJams Active Inventory	Inventory
iJams Customer Invoice	Customers
iJams Order Subform	Customers

9. Click the **Navigation Pane** title bar and choose **Show All** at the bottom of the menu to display all objects in their assigned groups, if necessary.

Setting Database Properties

Video Lesson   labyrinthelab.com/videos

Database properties are similar to object properties, but they define features of the database as a whole. You can set database properties to identify the database name and author and to add keywords for searches. You can also examine database properties to determine when it was created or last updated.

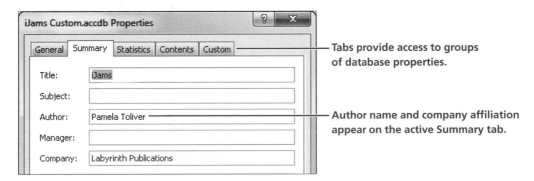

Tabs provide access to groups of database properties.

Author name and company affiliation appear on the active Summary tab.

Set Database Properties

In this exercise, you will change the company name to the name of your school and add your name as the database author.

1. Follow these steps to open the database Properties dialog box:

A Choose **File**.   **B** Click **Info**.   **C** Click the *View and edit database properties* hyperlink.

2. Click the **Summary** tab and **type** your name in the Author field.

3. **Type** your instructor's name in the Manager field.

4. **Type** the name of your school in the Company field.

5. Click **OK** to save the changes to the database properties.

Setting Up Current Database Format

Video Lesson   labyrinthelab.com/videos

Error-checking options you set earlier affect how Access works with every database you open or create. Current Database settings enable you to change the way Access displays and works with only the active database. You can, for example, change the text Access displays in the title bar when the database is open, show or hide the Navigation Pane, enable views, or change the way Access displays open objects.

Changing the Title Text in the Application Bar

Many times, the actual filename assigned to a database is different from the text you would like users to see when they open the database. You can change the text that appears in the title bar by typing the text in the Current Database options window.

Typing the text in the Application Title text box displays the title bar of the Access window when the database is open.

Setting Object Window Format

Most of the database objects you have used throughout this book were set to format as tabbed documents within the database work area. You can change the format for object windows to display as overlapping windows similar to what was used in previous versions of Access databases.

FROM THE KEYBOARD
Ctrl + F6 to navigate among open objects.

Overlapping windows have individual title bars that "float" in the work area window.

Tabs for tabbed documents align at the top of the work area.

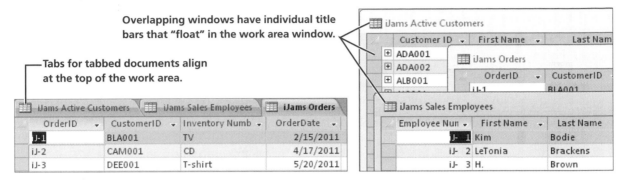

 After changing the document windows options, you must close and then reopen the database to view the new settings.

DEVELOP YOUR SKILLS 11.1.4

Set Current Database Options

In this exercise, you will change settings for the current database to edit the title and change the document window options.

1. Choose **File→Options** to display the Access Options dialog box.

2. Follow these steps to change the Application Title text and window display setting:

Ⓐ Choose **Current Database**.

Ⓑ Click the **Application Title** text box and type **iJams**.

Ⓒ Choose the **Overlapping Windows** option.

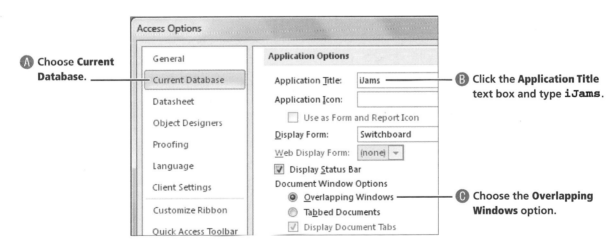

3. Explore other options available for the current database, and then click **OK**.
   Access displays a message advising you that you must close and then reopen the database for the settings to take effect.

4. Choose **OK** to acknowledge the message; then **close** and **reopen** the database.

5. Open the **iJams Active Customers** and **iJams Active Inventory** tables to display the objects in separate windows.

6. Drag the title bar of the **iJams Active Inventory** table window down to view the iJams Active Customers title bar.

7. **Close** ☒ both objects.

Setting Datasheet Colors and Default Font

Video Lesson   labyrinthelab.com/videos

Color can add character to database tables and other objects when they are displayed as datasheets. Tools for setting default font size and weight and gridline and cell effects are found in the Datasheet category of the Access Options dialog box. In addition, you can change the default color scheme that affects the display of database objects by selecting the color scheme from the General category.

QUICK REFERENCE	SETTING ACCESS OPTIONS
Task	**Procedure**
Enable error checking	■ Choose File→Options→Object Designers category. ■ Scroll to the bottom of the Access Options dialog box. ■ Click the Error indicator color menu and choose the appropriate color.
Create a Navigation Pane group	■ Choose File→Options→Current Database category. ■ Display the Navigation area. ■ Click the Navigation Options button and set up the group. *or* ■ Right-click the Navigation Pane title bar. ■ Select Navigation Options. ■ Set up the new group.
Assign objects to a Navigation Pane group	■ Display the Navigation Options and create a new group, if necessary. ■ Right-click the object to assign and choose Add to Group→Group Name.
Change the title case in the Application Bar	■ Choose File→Options→Current Database. ■ Click the Application Title text box and type the title text.
Set object window format	■ Choose File→Options→Current Database. ■ Choose the option for the window display to apply.
Set an Access color scheme	■ Choose File→Options→General category. ■ Click the list button for the Color Scheme setting and choose the color to apply.
Set a default font size and weight	■ Choose File→Options→Datasheet category. ■ Click the Size or Weight list button and choose the appropriate setting.
Set database properties	■ Choose File→Options to open the Properties dialog box and click the View and edit database properties hyperlink. ■ Click the tab containing the property you want to set. ■ Change the property, and then click OK.

Change Datasheet settings and Color Scheme

In this exercise, you will change the database color scheme and select font and gridline options for the datasheet.

1. Choose **File→Options** to open the Access Options dialog box.

2. Follow these steps to set font size, font weight, and cell effects for the datasheet:

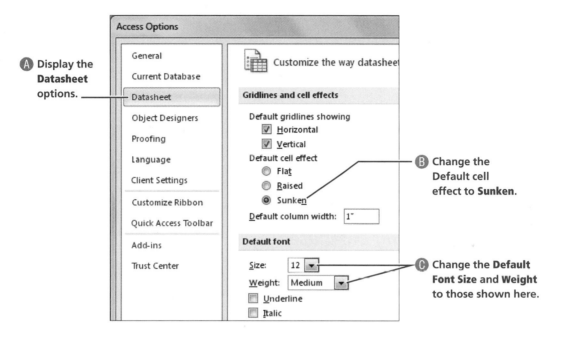

3. Follow these steps to change the color scheme for the database:

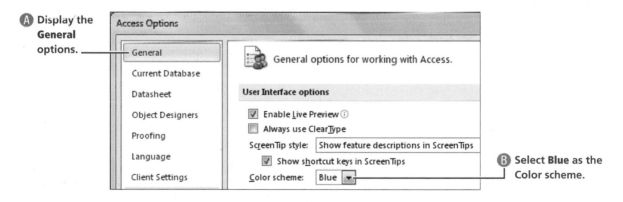

4. Click **OK** and then open the **iJams Active Customers** table to view the changes. *Your datasheet should resemble the following illustration.*

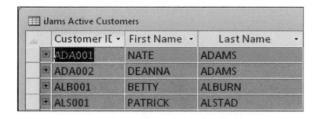

11.2 Customizing the Database Interface

Video Lesson   labyrinthelab.com/videos

Customizing the database interface is what makes an Access database easier for novice data entry people to use. It actually lets them click a button to perform actions that they have rights to perform. In this section, you will learn how to customize the interface and set up a switchboard as well as a Navigation Form.

Splitting a Database

Most databases provide queries, forms, reports, and other objects that data-entry personnel use to perform tasks associated with the database. Although these objects are designed to optimize data input and to extract the table records that answer common questions, individual users sometimes like to edit the design and layout of these objects and develop their own objects to meet their needs. For example, suppose an order-processing clerk is asked to retrieve a list of colors associated with a company's most popular line of draperies and must develop a query to search the database for the information each time a customer asks for the information. The clerk may want to develop and save a query as part of the database and run the query to retrieve the data more quickly.

Risks of Splitting Databases

Allowing users to create untold numbers of objects and add those objects to the database could potentially overwhelm the database with non-standard, single-use, untested, and unapproved objects. These objects increase the chance of data corruption and sometimes disconnect database relationships. To guard the data contained in database tables from becoming corrupt, most companies secure their databases, which prevents users from developing and saving new objects. One alternate solution that protects table data while enabling users to create and customize objects to meet their personal needs is to split the database.

Using the Database Splitter

The database splitter converts a database into two files—one that contains the tables holding the data that support all other database objects and one that contains the database reports, forms, queries, and other objects that use the data. After splitting the database, users in a networked environment—where multiple users access the database at the same time—can design and modify their own database objects without increasing the number of objects contained in the whole database. As a result, each user can access, edit, and update table data from the database tables without interrupting other users.

Identifying Split Database Terminology

Two terms are often associated with split databases:

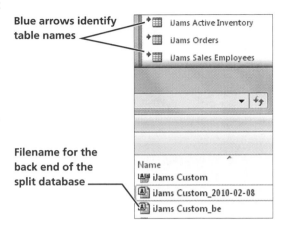

Blue arrows identify table names

- **Front-end** identifies the portion of a split data-base with which users interact—the forms, reports, etc., that they use and can also create. It's the portion of the database that appears up front where they can use it. Access places a blue arrow beside each table name in a split database to identify objects that users can view but not change.

Filename for the back end of the split database

- **Back-end** refers to the tables that support the front-end. Access adds _be to the end of the back-end portion of the database filename.

When you split a database, Access creates a link between the front-end and back-end of the database so that users can select field controls on forms, queries, and reports they create.

Backing Up a Database Prior to Splitting

Access recommends that you back up a database before you split it to preserve the database as a single file in case an error occurs during the splitting process.

QUICK REFERENCE	SPLITTING A DATABASE
Task	**Procedure**
Split a database	■ Choose Database Tools→Move Data→Access Database from the Ribbon to launch the Database Splitter. ■ Click the Split Database button. ■ Open the destination folder for the split database, and then click Split.

DEVELOP YOUR SKILLS 11.2.1
Split a Database

In this exercise, you will create a backup of the database and then use the Database Splitter feature to split the iJams database.

Before You Begin: Your iJams database should be open.

1. **Close** ✕ all open database objects, and then choose **File→Save & Publish→Back Up Database** to open the Save As dialog box.

2. **Open** the folder in which you are storing your data files and then click **Save** to save the backup using the default filename Access assigns.

3. Choose **Database Tools→Move Data→Access Database** to launch the Database Splitter.

4. Review the information displayed in the Database Splitter window and then click the **Split Database** button.
   Access opens the Create Back-end Database dialog box and displays the name of the file it will create during the split.

5. **Navigate** to the folder in which you are storing your data files and then click **Split**.
   Access displays a message box when the split is complete.

6. Click **OK** to acknowledge the message.

7. Follow these steps to review the results of the split:

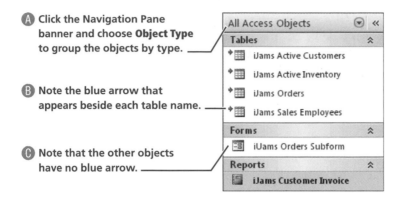

A Click the Navigation Pane banner and choose **Object Type** to group the objects by type.

B Note the blue arrow that appears beside each table name.

C Note that the other objects have no blue arrow.

8. **Close** the database.

Creating a Database Switchboard

Video Lesson   labyrinthelab.com/videos

A *database switchboard* contains menus and buttons for opening database objects and performing common tasks such as adding records, printing reports, and so forth. Creating a switchboard makes the database more user-friendly—especially when those who use the database have limited database experience. In essence, a switchboard is a form that you can create from scratch or by using an Access feature called the Switchboard Manager. When you use the Switchboard Manager to create the switchboard, Access creates a form named Switchboard. You can set tasks you want to display on the Switchboard form so that users can click the task button to open the database object that they need to complete the task. The switchboard sits between the database and the user as an easy-to-use interface.

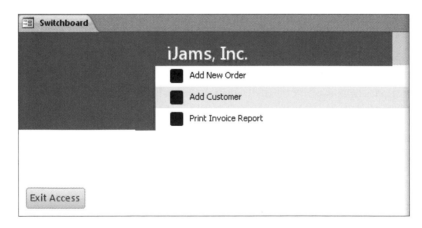

A sample database switchboard

Adding Switchboard Tool to the Ribbon

In order to create a Switchboard in Access 2010, the Switchboard button must be added to the Ribbon. To customize the Ribbon, you must first select the tab of the Ribbon on which you want to place the button, and then create a group to hold the button. You cannot add a button to an existing Ribbon group. The Ribbon can be customized without opening a database.

The database Switchboard Manager button will appear on the Access 2010 Database Tools tab of the Ribbon if you open a database created in a previous version of Access or one created by someone else that already contains a database Switchboard. If you find the Switchboard Manager button already available in Access, skip Develop Your Skills and continue with the next topic.

DEVELOP YOUR SKILLS 11.2.2
Add Switchboard Button to the Ribbon

In this exercise, you will customize the Database Tools Ribbon by adding the Switchboard button.

1. In Access, click the **Database Tools** tab on the Ribbon to make it active.

2. **Right-click** the Database Tools Ribbon and choose **Customize the Ribbon**.
   Access opens the Access Options dialog box with the Customize Ribbon options displayed and the Database Tools group selected.

3. Follow these steps to add a new group to the Database Tools Ribbon:

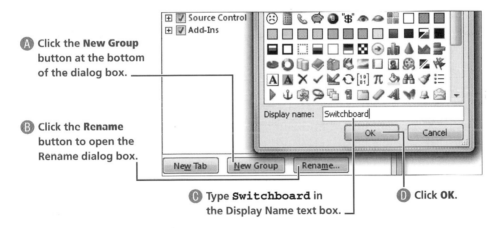

Ⓐ Click the **New Group** button at the bottom of the dialog box.

Ⓑ Click the **Rename** button to open the Rename dialog box.

Ⓒ Type **Switchboard** in the Display Name text box.

Ⓓ Click **OK**.

4. Follow these steps to add the Switchboard Manager button to the new group:

Ⓐ Select **Commands Not in the Ribbon** from the Choose Commands From list.

Ⓑ Scroll down the list and select **Switchboard Manager**.

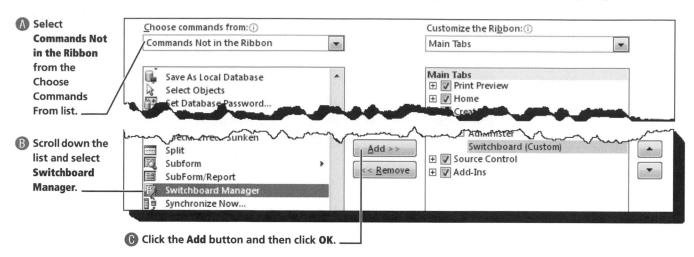

Ⓒ Click the **Add** button and then click **OK**.

Access places the button in the new group.

5. Click the **Database Tools** tab to view the new group.

Adding Items to a Switchboard

Video Lesson   labyrinthelab.com/videos

Each database you create contains a Main Switchboard object that remains hidden until you customize it and make it active. As a result, you will actually be modifying an existing object when you create your switchboard. Using the tools in Access, you can add only those objects and links to the switchboard that enable users to perform the tasks they need to accomplish.

Identifying the Switchboard Items Table

When you create a switchboard and add commands to the switchboard using the Switchboard Manager, Access creates a new table in the database and places a list of the commands required to perform the common tasks in the table. You can open the Switchboard Items table, modify the arrangement of items on the switchboard, edit items, add additional items, and so forth.

QUICK REFERENCE	CREATING A SWITCHBOARD
Task	**Procedure**
Create a main switchboard	■ Add the Switchboard Manager button to the Ribbon.
	■ Choose Database Tools→Switchboard→Switchboard Manager ⧉ from the Ribbon.
	■ Respond to the message to create a switchboard now.
	■ Select the Main Switchboard item, and then click the Edit button.
	■ Click New to create a new action item on the form and complete the text boxes to identify the action and other required data about the item.
	■ Click OK.

Create a Database Switchboard

In this exercise, you will create a switchboard using the Switchboard Manager.

1. **Open** the iJams Interface database and **save** it as a new database named **iJams Navigation**.

2. Choose **Database Tools→Switchboard→Switchboard Manager** 📝 from the Ribbon.
   Access opens the Switchboard Manager dialog box and selects the Main Switchboard (Default) item in the list.

3. Choose **Yes** to tell Access that you want to create one now.

4. Follow these steps to create and add an item to the Switchboard:

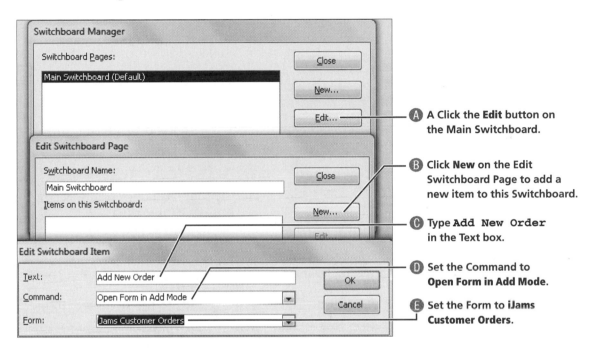

A Click the **Edit** button on the Main Switchboard.

B Click **New** on the Edit Switchboard Page to add a new item to this Switchboard.

C Type **Add New Order** in the Text box.

D Set the Command to **Open Form in Add Mode**.

E Set the Form to **iJams Customer Orders**.

5. Click **OK** and then repeat the procedures outlined in **step 3: B-E** to create the following additional items on the Switchboard:

Text	Command	Object
Add Customer	Open Form in Add Mode	iJams Customer Orders
Print Invoice Report	Open Report	iJams Customer Invoice

6. Click **Close** to close the Edit Switchboard Page dialog box, and then click **Close** again to close the Switchboard Manager dialog box.
   Access creates two new objects: A new table named Switchboard Items and a new form named Switchboard. To ensure that the commands on the Switchboard work properly, you will now test the controls.

Test the Switchboard

7. Open the **Switchboard** form and review the form.
Your form should resemble the following illustration.

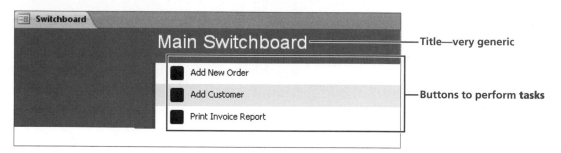

8. Click the **Add New Order** button and ensure that the iJams Customer Orders form opens.

9. **Close** ☒ the form and then click the **Add Customer** button on the Switchboard to open the iJams Customer Orders form.

10. **Close** ☒ the form and then click the **Print Invoice Report** to open the iJams Customer Invoice report.

11. **Close** ☒ the report and then **close** ☒ the Switchboard form.

Adding Custom Command Buttons to a Switchboard

Video Lesson   labyrinthelab.com/videos

By the time you are ready to create a switchboard form, most, if not all, database objects required to enter data into database tables, query the database, and report database data are complete. When you create the switchboard, the buttons and tasks listed on the switchboard are linked to other database objects that allow users access to the objects so they can complete their tasks. Adding commands using the Switchboard Manager creates small buttons and places text to the side of the buttons on the switchboard form. You can create buttons in the form Design View by creating a command button. One advantage to adding command buttons manually is that you can size and position the button where you want it on the form and add text directly onto the button. Another advantage to creating buttons manually is that you have a larger selection of actions that you can attach to a button.

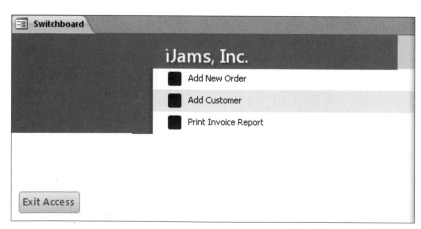

A button is added to the form to exit Access when work is completed.

When you use the Command Button control on the Ribbon to create a command button, the Command Button Wizard opens and walks you through the process of setting a button action. Command buttons such as the one pictured above appear in the Form Footer section. Placing the buttons in the Detail section would replicate the button for each entry in the form.

QUICK REFERENCE	CREATING ACTION BUTTONS ON FORMS
Task	**Procedure**
Create an action button on a database object	■ Choose Design→Controls→Button XXXX from the Ribbon and draw a button in the appropriate position.
	■ Follow the Wizard prompts to make the desired settings for the button.
	■ Click Finish.

DEVELOP YOUR SKILLS 11.2.4
Add Command Buttons to a Switchboard

In this exercise, you will create a command button on the Switchboard form in the database, add text to the button, and attach a command to the button. In addition, you will edit the title of the form.

Before You Begin: Your iJams Navigation database should be open.

1. Open the **Switchboard Items** table, and then follow these steps to edit the form title:

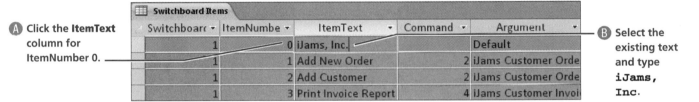

Ⓐ Click the **ItemText** column for ItemNumber 0.

Ⓑ Select the existing text and type **iJams, Inc.**

2. **Close** ✕ the table, and then display the Switchboard form in **Design View**.

3. Expand the **Form Footer** area by dragging the bottom of the form down.

4. Choose **Design→Controls→Button** XXXX from the Ribbon and draw a button in the Form Footer section, as shown in the illustration to the right.

Access numbers command buttons sequentially. As a result, the number you see on the command button may be different from the one shown here.

Access launches the Command Button Wizard after you draw the command button.

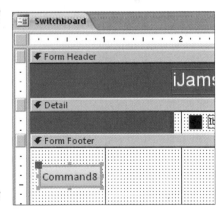

5. Follow these steps to complete the first button:

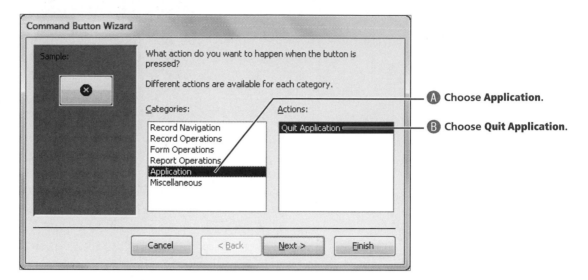

A Choose **Application**.

B Choose **Quit Application**.

6. Click next and follow these steps to complete the button:

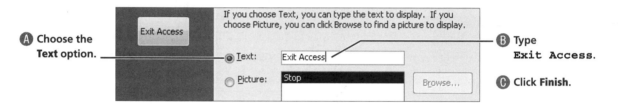

A Choose the Text option.

B Type **Exit Access**.

C Click **Finish**.

Access places the text on the button. Now you will test the button.

7. **Save** 💾 changes to the form and then switch to **Form View**.

8. Click the **Exit Access** button on the form.
The database and Access both close.

Creating a Navigation Form

Video Lesson labyrinthelab.com/videos

With the advent of Office 2010, Microsoft implemented a large push to make creating databases that work on the Web more efficient. After reviewing numerous Web pages, the company built a series of forms that introduce the layouts most frequently found on popular sites and called these forms Navigation Forms.

Identifying Navigation Form Features

Navigation Forms have tabs across the top of the form for grouping common elements for easy navigation commands with sub-navigation links directly below or along the left side of the form. Navigation Forms provide an alternative way to build a user interface to access tools for performing common tasks. It also provides a way to view data online from one working window so that users have no need to search through numerous forms and report layouts to locate the one they need.

─The Navigation Form tab opens like a form in the work area of the Access window.

Navigation Form

| Order Processing | Customers | Reports | Sales Force | [Add New] |

iJams Customer Orders | iJams Customers

─Individual objects can be accessed using navigation controls on the side of an active tab.

Tabs within the form group database objects by type. You can drag forms and reports to the tab area at the top or side of the form.

When you create a tab that matches the name of a form or report in the database, Access automatically assigns the form or report to the tab in the Navigation Form.

Getting Ready to Create a Navigation Form

Navigation Forms can hold forms and reports. As a result, careful planning is often required before actually creating a Navigation Form. Recall that split databases are often set up to prevent data corruption but enable users to create forms, queries, and reports based on those tables. Using tables in a split database to create forms that display the table data is a good way to access table data from within the Navigation Form work area. Setting the form to display data in datasheet layout makes using sort and filter, find and replace, and other tools more efficient than single forms.

DEVELOP YOUR SKILLS 11.2.5
Create New Forms

In this exercise, you will create two new forms: one to display Customers and one to display Sales Employees in Datasheet layout.

1. **Launch** Access and **open** the iJams Navigation database and **display** the Navigation Pane.

2. Select the **iJams Customers** table without opening it and choose **Create→Forms→ Form** to create a new form.

3. Display the new form in **Design View** and delete the **subform control** at the bottom of the window.

4. Display the **Property Sheet** for the form and change the Default View property to **Datasheet**.

5. **Save** the form using the default form name.

6. Repeat the procedures outlined in **steps 2 through 5** to create a form and set the Datasheet View for the iJams Sales Employees table, saving the table using the default name.

7. **Close** both forms and then **open** them again to ensure that they display as Datasheets.

Locating Navigation Form Layouts

Video Lesson labyrinthelab.com/videos

Now that you have the forms needed to place on the Navigation Form, you can begin building the form. As a database grows, additional forms and reports can be added to the Navigation Form to make them easily accessible. Access provides a palette of six different Navigation Form layouts from which you can choose.

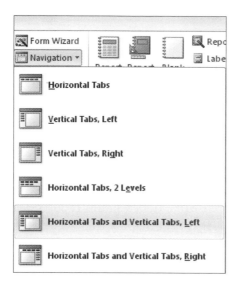

DEVELOP YOUR SKILLS 11.2.6
Create a Navigation Form

In this exercise, you will create a new Navigation Form and add tabs and database objects to the form.
Before You Begin: Your iJams Navigation database should be open.

1. Follow these steps to create a new Navigation Form:

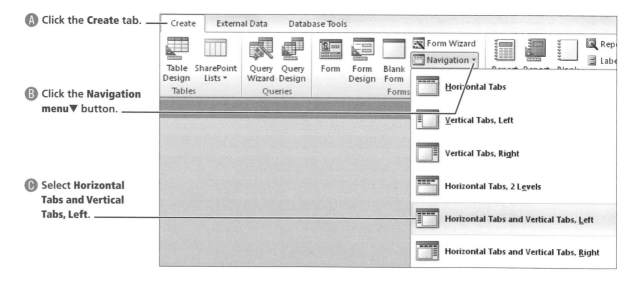

Ⓐ Click the **Create tab.**

Ⓑ Click the **Navigation menu▼** button.

Ⓒ Select **Horizontal Tabs and Vertical Tabs, Left.**

2. **Double-click** the [Add New] tab at the top of the form and type **Order Processing**, as shown here.

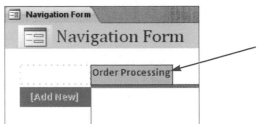

3. **Press** [Enter] and then follow these steps to size the tab:

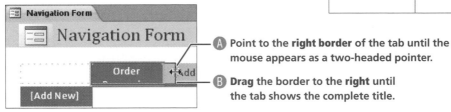

(A) Point to the **right border** of the tab until the mouse appears as a two-headed pointer.

(B) **Drag** the border to the **right** until the tab shows the complete title.

4. Repeat the procedures outlined in **step 2** to create additional tabs for the following three items: **Customers, Reports, Sales Force**.

Add Items to Tabs

5. Follow these steps to add an item to a tab:

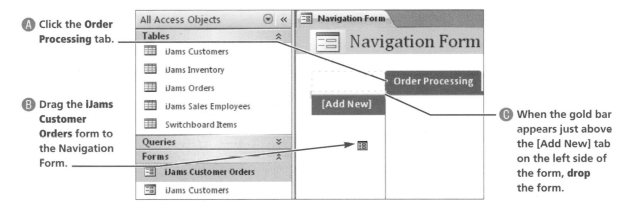

(A) Click the **Order Processing** tab.

(B) Drag the **iJams Customer Orders** form to the Navigation Form.

(C) When the gold bar appears just above the [Add New] tab on the left side of the form, **drop** the form.

6. Repeat the procedures outlined in **step 5** to add the following forms to the tab indicated:

Tab	Form or Report
Customers	iJams Customers
Reports	iJams Customer Invoice
Sales Force	iJams Sales Employees

7. **Save** the form as iJams, Inc and then display the form in **Design View**.
   Notice that there is no period following Inc—Access does not accept periods in object names. On the other hand, title text added to forms can include a period.

8. Change the title on the form to **iJams, Inc.**

9. Add the **iJams logo** to the Form Header section and set the Size Mode property to **Stretch**.

10. Switch to **Form View**, **close** the Navigation Pane, and view the completed form.

Setting Startup Options to Open a Form

Video Lesson   labyrinthelab.com/videos

Switchboards and Navigation Forms provide an interface between the user and other objects contained in the database. In most instances, those who use the database to enter and edit data, generate reports, and locate information have no reason to see the Navigation Pane, create objects, or modify the design of existing objects. Their job is simply to process data.

As a result, many businesses set startup options that display the database interface so that it is the first thing a user sees when they open the database. Setting these startup options is another way to protect the database against unauthorized access.

Overriding Startup Options

FROM THE KEYBOARD

Shift (press and hold as you open a database) to override startup options

After you set startup options for a database, you may wonder how you are to access the database features that may be hidden. When startup options hide the Navigation Pane, for example, you can override the startup options as you open the database. To override the settings, press and hold the Shift key as you open the database in Access.

QUICK REFERENCE	SETTING A SWITCHBOARD AS A STARTUP FORM
Task	**Procedure**
Set a startup form	■ Choose File→Options→Current Database.
	■ Click the Display Form list button and choose the form you want to set as the startup form.
	■ Click OK.

DEVELOP YOUR SKILLS 11.2.7
Set a Startup Form

In this exercise, you will set the Switchboard form to open automatically each time you open the database.
Before You Begin: Your iJams Navigation database should be open.

1. Choose **File→Options→Current Database**.

2. Click the **Display** Form list button and choose **Switchboard** as the startup form.

3. Click **OK** to close the Access Options dialog box.

4. Click **OK** to acknowledge the message box.

5. **Close** the database and **open** it again.
   Access opens the database and displays the Switchboard form.

6. **Close** ☒ the form and then **close** the database.

11.3 Setting Database Security

Video Lesson   labyrinthelab.com/videos

Imagine that your medical records are all stored in a large database that is accessible to all hospitals, clinics, and medical insurance companies along with anyone else who wants to know more about the medications you take and when your last checkup was. Databases, by nature, often hold confidential information that needs to be kept private. As a result, security is an important element. Companies that maintain large database files often set access to databases at the login or server level. Splitting a database also protects the data contained in databases. In addition, Access contains features that enable you to secure a database by assigning a password.

Opening a Database Exclusively

Most databases for large businesses are designed to enable multiple users access to the database at the same time. As a result, the default setting for databases is as shared files. Before you can set security for a database, you must first ensure that no one else is using the database. You do this by opening the file exclusively so that Access locks the database and prevents others from accessing it while you set security.

Opening Database Commands

Access contains numerous commands for opening databases. You can simply click the Open button in the Open dialog box after selecting a file to open and Access opens the database. In addition, you can choose an open command that is designed to control the types of activities available while you have the database open. The following table identifies and describes when you should use each command on the Open drop-down list.

QUICK REFERENCE	OPENING DATABASE COMMANDS
Command	**Description**
Open	Provides full access to the database, its objects, and menus. When you open the database, you can edit data, create objects, delete objects, and perform other functions on the database.
Open Read Only	Opens the database with a message bar at the top of the window that advises you that you can only change data in linked tables. You can also view and print data from the database. To make design changes, you would need to save the database as a new file.
Open Exclusive	Opens the database and locks it to prevent other users in a shared environment from accessing the database.
Open Exclusive Read-Only	Opens the database and locks it so other users cannot access it and prevents edits to data and database objects.

Open a Database for Exclusive Use

In this exercise, you will open the iJams Navigation database exclusively.

Before You Begin: All databases should be closed.

1. Choose **File→Open** and navigate to the folder containing your iJams Navigation database.

2. **Click** the database filename (without double-clicking) to select it.

3. Follow these steps to open the database in exclusive mode:

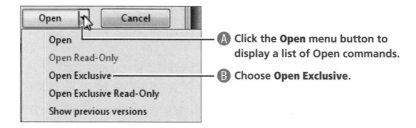

Ⓐ Click the **Open** menu button to display a list of Open commands.

Ⓑ Choose **Open Exclusive**.

4. **Enable content**, if necessary.

Encrypting a Database Using a Password

Video Lesson   labyrinthelab.com/videos

Regardless of whether a backup routine is in place to save files regularly outside the main computer server, valuable time can be lost reconstructing orders and other data if unauthorized users sabotage the database. Database passwords act like passwords you use to access bank accounts or email and are meant to be kept confidential. Only those who should be allowed to access a database should be given the password.

Identifying Limits of Passwords

Database passwords provide limited security for databases by preventing unauthorized users from opening the database. You can set a password for any database you have on your personal computer just as systems administrators set a password for shared databases on a network. However, if a database is already open on a computer, no other security measures are provided unless higher-level security measures (such as user-level security or security account passwords set by an administrator) are also set.

Passwords are case sensitive—capable of distinguishing between uppercase and lowercase letters. Access remembers which characters you typed in capital letters and which characters you typed in lower-case.

Creating Strong Passwords

Strong passwords use a combination of upper- and lower-case characters, symbols, and numbers. Access allows any combination of characters *except* " \ [ ] : | < > + = ; , . ? and * to be used in passwords. Passwords may not start with a space. Although the password you will use for this lesson is an easy password, it is one that is uniform and easy to remember.

Strong Password Example: 20Access10#1

Weak Password Example: Access2010

Setting Up Databases for Assigning Passwords

To assign a database password, the database must initially be closed. The default access setting for databases that appear on a network is as a shared database. To set a password, you must open the database with *exclusive access* using the Open Exclusive command in the Open dialog box. This ensures that no one else is currently using the database.

The Encrypt with Password command on the File menu is a toggle command. When a database is protected with a password, the command button shows Decrypt Database.

QUICK REFERENCE	SETTING AND REMOVING A DATABASE PASSWORD
Task	**Procedure**
Set a password	■ Open the database in exclusive mode.
	■ Choose File→Info→Encrypt with Password.
	■ Type the password to assign in the Password textbox.
	■ Type the password again in the Verify textbox.
	■ Click OK.
Remove a password	■ Open the database in exclusive mode.
	■ Choose File→Info→Decrypt Database.
	■ Type the password in the Password box, and then click OK.

Set a Database Password

In this exercise, you will set a database password to protect the database so that no one can access it from your workstation.

Before You Begin: Your iJams Navigation database should be open in exclusive mode.

1. Choose **File→Info→Encrypt with Password**.

2. Follow these steps to set the password:

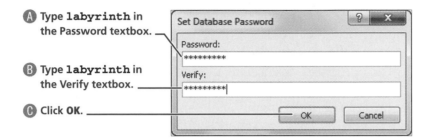

Ⓐ Type **labyrinth** in the Password textbox.

Ⓑ Type **labyrinth** in the Verify textbox.

Ⓒ Click **OK**.

*Access displays asterisks (*) in the textboxes as you type.*

3. Click **OK** to acknowledge the message, **close** the database, and **open** it again.
   Access displays the Password Required dialog box.

4. Type **labyrinth** in the Enter Database Password textbox, and then click **OK** to open the database.

5. **Close** the database.

11.4 Concepts Review

Concepts Review   labyrinthelab.com/acc10

To check your knowledge of the key concepts introduced in this lesson, complete the Concepts Review quiz by going to the URL listed above. If your classroom is using Labyrinth eLab, you may complete the Concepts Review quiz from within your eLab course.

Reinforce Your Skills

Split a Database

The Flower Pot flower shop is getting ready to go live with its new database. As a result, they need to finish the customization and set up security. In this exercise, you will split the database to create a back-end database to protect the tables in the database.

1. **Open** the rs-Flower Pot database and **save** the database in the trusted folder containing your student files using the new database name **rs-Flower Pot Custom**.

2. Choose **Database Tools→Move Data→Access Database** [icon] to launch the Database Splitter.

3. Click the **Split Database** button.

4. Open the **trusted folder**, and then click **Split** to create the back-end file using the **filename** Access assigns.

5. Click **OK** to acknowledge the message and review the Navigation Pane.

Create a Switchboard and Add Command Buttons

A switchboard will make the database more user-friendly for Flower Pot staff. In this exercise, you will create a switchboard using the Switchboard Manager and add a command button to the switchboard. When you are finished, your switchboard should resemble the following illustration.

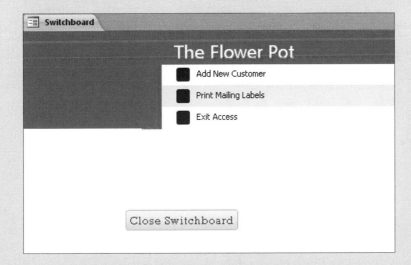

Before You Begin: Your rs-The Flower Pot Custom database should be open.

1. Choose **Database Tools→Database Tools→Switchboard Manager** .

2. Choose **Yes** in response to the message box asking if you want to create a switchboard now.

3. Click the **Main Switchboard** item in the Switchboard Manager window, and then click the **Edit** button.

4. Click the **New** button, and then enter the following items individually to the switchboard:

Text	Command	Object
Add New Customer	Open Form in Add Mode	The Flower Pot Customers
Print Mailing Labels	Open Report	Labels Flower Pot Customers
Exit Access	Exit Application	N/A

5. Close the **Edit Switchboard Page**, and then close the **Switchboard Manager**.

Edit the Switchboard Title

6. Open the **Switchboard Items** table and edit the ItemText for the first item (0) by typing **The Flower Pot**.

7. **Close** ☒ the table, and then **open** the Switchboard form.

Test the Buttons

8. **Click** each control button to determine if they are working properly.

REINFORCE YOUR SKILLS 11.3

Add a Command Button to a Form

In this exercise, you will add a command button to the Switchboard form and test the button to ensure that it works.

1. Display the Switchboard form in **Design View**.

2. Expand the **Form Footer** area and choose **Design→Controls→Button** xxxx .

3. Draw a **button** below the switchboard buttons as shown on the Switchboard illustration.

4. Set the commands using the Command Button Wizard as follows:
   - **Categories:** Form Operations
   - **Action:** Close Form
   - **Text to appear on button:** Close Switchboard

Test the Button

5. **Save** changes to the form and then switch to **Form View**.

6. Click the **Close Switchboard** button.
   Access closes the Switchboard form.

Create a Navigation Form

The Flower Pot is exploring the possibility of using a Navigation Form instead of a Switchboard for data entry. In this exercise, you will create a Navigation Form for the company so that it can determine which form it wants to implement as a startup form.

Before You Begin: Your rs-The Flower Pot Custom database should be open.

1. Select the **Departments** table and choose **Create→Forms→Form** to create a generic form for the table.

2. **Save** the form using the default name Access applies and **open** the new form in **Design View**.

3. Display the **Property Sheet** and set the Default View to **Datasheet**.

4. **Save** changes to the form and **close** it.

5. Choose **Create→Forms→Navigation** and select **Horizontal Tabs, 2 Levels**.

6. **Double-click** the top [Add New] tab and create individual tabs for the following groups: Departments, Customers, Labels.

7. **Save** the Navigation Form and then click the **Departments** tab and review the data, adjusting column width to show all data.

8. Click the **Customers** tab and drag The Flower Pot Customers form to the second level [Add New] below the tab.

9. Click the **Labels** tab and drag the Labels Flower Pot Customers report to the second level below the tab.

10. Review all tabs of data, **save** changes to the form, and **print** a copy of the form.

Set Database Options

Now that you have the switchboard set to contain the tasks users need to complete, you can set database options. In this exercise, you will set the switchboard to open when users open the database, hide the Navigation Pane, and change the text that appears in the database application title bar.

Before You Begin: Your rs-The Flower Pot Custom database should be open.

1. Choose **File→Options→Current Database**.

2. Type **The Flower Pot** in the Application Title text box.

3. **Clear** the checkmark from the Display Navigation Pane checkbox.

4. Click the **Display Form** list button and choose **Switchboard**.

5. Click **OK** to save the settings and then **close** the database.

Test the Settings

6. **Open** the database again to view the switchboard without the Navigation Pane.

7. **Close** the database again and then **press** Shift and hold it down while you **open** the database one more time.

8. Open the **Departments** table and review the datasheet.

9. **Close** ☒ the table and then **close** the database.

REINFORCE YOUR SKILLS 11.6
Encrypt with a Password

To ensure that only authorized users open the database, you need to set a password. In this exercise, you will set a password for the database.

1. Choose **File→Open** and navigate to the Lesson 11 folder.

2. **Click** the rs-The Flower Pot Custom database to select it.

3. Click the **Open** button list button and choose **Open Exclusive**.

4. Choose **File→Info→Encrypt with Password** 🔳.

5. Type **flowers** in the Password text box and then type **flowers** again in the Verify text box.

6. Choose **OK** and then **close** the database.

7. **Open** the database again, **type** the password when prompted, and click **OK**.

Apply Your Skills

Create a Client-Friendly User Interface

Brokers at Homestead-Properties realty company want to set up their database at a kiosk so that people can access information about the homes they have listed for sale. Such a setup would enable potential clients as well as the general public to locate data about listings when the company offices are closed. In this exercise, you will split the database to prevent people from accessing database tables and then set up a switchboard that allows people to search the database by address and price. After you complete the switchboard, you will change the startup options to control access to other features in the front-end file. A sample of the database switchboard appears in the following illustration. The switchboard you design may be different.

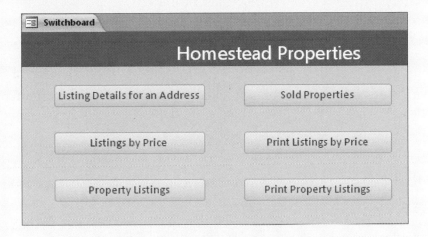

1. **Open** the as-Homestead Properties database from the Lesson 11 folder and **save** it as a new file named **as-Homestead Properties Custom**.

2. **Split** the database, **saving** the back-end file using the filename Access assigns.

3. Create a **new switchboard** but add no actions.

4. Display the Switchboard form in **Design View** and **delete** the controls Access placed in the Detail section, including the graphics boxes.

5. Make the **Form Header** section larger and add **command buttons** to the Form Header section of the form for each task shown in the following list:

- A button containing the text **Listing Details for an Address** that performs a report operation to preview the Property Listing by Address report
- A button containing the text **Property Listings by Price** to preview the Property Listings by Price report
- A button containing the text **Homestead Property Listings** to preview the Active Listings report
- A button containing the text **Sold Homestead Properties** to preview the Sold Homestead Properties report
- A button containing the text **Print Listings by Price** that prints a copy of the Property Listings by Price report
- A button containing the text **Print Homestead Property Listings** that prints a copy of the Active Listings report

6. Align and position buttons appropriately, narrow the height of the Detail and Form Footer sections, and expand the Form Header section to the bottom of the window.

7. Change the title of the form to **Homestead Properties** in the Switchboard Items table.

8. Switch to **Form View** and test each button, **closing** each database objects after you verify that it is correct.

9. **Close** the database.

Create a Navigation Form

Homestead Properties would also like to create a Navigation Form for people at the office to use with the database. In this exercise, you will design a Navigation Form for Homestead Properties in the as-Homestead Properties Custom database.

Before You Begin: Your as-Homestead Properties Custom database should be open.

1. Create a new **Navigation Form** using the Horizontal Tabs and Vertical Tabs, Right layout.

2. Create **tabs** across the top of the form for the following groups: Listings, Reports.

3. Add appropriate **reports** in the database to the Reports tab.

4. Add appropriate **forms** in the database to the Listings tab.

5. **Save** the Navigation Form using the form name Homestead Properties and **print** a copy of each form page.

Change the Title Text and Set Security

Only authorized people at Homestead Properties can add and edit listings for properties in the database. In this exercise, you will set a database password for the database to ensure that only authorized users access the database to add records, edit data, and delete records. In addition, you will set title text for the database, hide the Navigation Pane, and set a startup form.

1. **Open** the as-Homestead Properties Custom database and encrypt it with the password **homes**.

2. Change the title text for the application to **Homestead Properties**.

3. Hide the **Navigation Pane** and change the form that displays when you open the database to show the **Switchboard**.

4. **Close** the database and then **exit** Access.

Critical Thinking & Work-Readiness Skills

In the course of working through the following Microsoft Office-based Critical Thinking exercises, you will also be utilizing various work-readiness skills, some of which are listed next to each exercise. Go to labyrinthelab.com/workreadiness *to learn more about the work-readiness skills.*

11.1 Create and Set Up a User Interface

WORK-READINESS SKILLS APPLIED

- Thinking creatively
- Making decisions
- Improving or designing systems

Foxy's gym has contracted for your help to implement a user interface the payroll clerk can use to add new employees, enter hours worked, preview and print pay stubs, and preview and print a personnel roster. They are trying to determine whether to use a Navigation Form or a Switchboard and want to design both forms in their database to help them determine which interface to use. Use ct-Foxy Gym (Lesson 11 folder) to create a new database named **ct-Foxy Gym Interface**. Use the new database to create the forms. After designing both forms, determine which one would make the better interface for Foxy's Payroll department and set it to open automatically when the database is used. Be prepared to demonstrate your database forms in class and defend your decision. Print copies of both forms.

11.2 Explore Access Options

WORK-READINESS SKILLS APPLIED

- Seeing things in the mind's eye
- Selecting technology
- Reasoning

The number of options available in the Access Options dialog box is extensive. Display the dialog box and review features available for each group. Then determine which features you would customize if you were designing a database to be used by people in your area of study. Compile the list in a Word document named **ct-Access Options** saved to your Lesson 11 folder. Explain why you would change the settings. Identify each setting as either an Access setting or a database setting.

11.3 Rethink the Navigation Pane

WORK-READINESS SKILLS APPLIED

- Improving or designing systems
- Thinking creatively
- Speaking

The Navigation Pane in Access databases can be customized to display groups of items differently from the standard display. Explore features and options of the Navigation Pane and determine how it might be customized to serve as a user interface. Then use the ct-Foxy Gym database (Lesson 11 folder) to create a new database named **ct-Foxy Gym Navigation** and customize the Navigation Pane appropriately. If working in a group, present your customizations and explain your decisions. If working alone, type your responses in a Word document named **ct-Navigation Pane** saved to your Lesson 11 folder. If time permits, search the Internet for samples of databases and templates that implement unique or creative user interface designs and download the samples to review with the class.

Integrating Access with Other Applications

LEARNING OBJECTIVES

After studying this lesson, you will be able to:

- Convert Access 2010 files to previous Access formats
- Share Access data with Word, Excel, and Outlook
- Work with HTML files

Through the last two decades, technology has improved, and a new electronic information age has evolved. Today, data is stored on all types of computer systems in a variety of formats throughout the world. Maintaining files and other data so that they are easy to share with others has become a greater challenge. Improvements in file formats such as XML have helped resolve data sharing. Access contains tools that make it easier than ever to import, export, and format files so you can share them with others. The tool you use and the format you choose for your data depends on who will view it, where they will view it, and how they plan to use it.

In this lesson, you will explore the numerous ways of sharing Access data with other Microsoft Office programs as well as identify ways and tools to use when you need to format data for other systems and for the web.

Sharing Data with Others

The iJams database stores all data related to customers, suppliers, orders, and employees. Having all the data stored together in one electronic file makes it more convenient for sharing with others in the company who need to use the data for mailings, invoices, posting to Web sites, connecting via email, and many other purposes. In some cases, the data can be used in its standard form—as part of an Access database. Sometimes, however, the data contained in the database needs to be exported from Access into another format so that it can be used. Exploring techniques for sharing Access data before it is actually needed will enable management at iJams to better prepare for how it will use the data in the future.

Aurelia Gonzalez, administrative assistant to the president, is working with Jamal Lawrence, webmaster, and Jin Chen, marketing analyst, to experiment with file formats to determine how to make the best use of the data. They want to create the following:

Access data exported to a Word document

Access data merged with a Word document

Access inventory data exported to Excel

Access customer orders exported in HTML format

A hyperlink added to an Access form

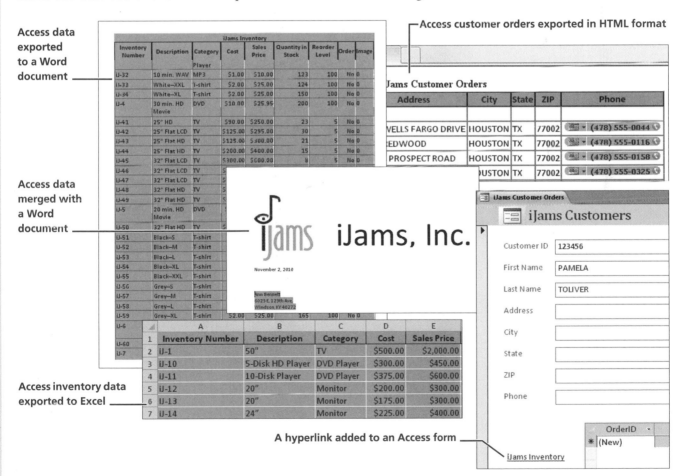

12.1 Converting Access 2010 Databases to Other Access Formats

Video Lesson labyrinthelab.com/videos

As you have already discovered, Access 2010 databases carry a unique format that is incompatible with previous versions of Microsoft Access. The main difference is, of course, the filename extension. Versions of Access prior to 2007 created files containing an .mdb extension. Access 2007 and 2010 create files containing an .accdb extension (for Access Database). As a result, to share an Access 2010 database with users who have Access 2000 or Access 2002–2003, you must save the database in a format that those versions recognize, using the Access 2010 Save & Publish command.

Identifying the Format of an Access Database

When you open a database in Access, Access identifies the version of the file in the title bar. For example, when you open a database created in Access 2007 or 2010, the name of the database along with "Database (Access 2007)" appears in the title bar unless you have changed the text to appear in the application title bar. When you open a file created or formatted for a previous version of Access, such as Access 2002–2003, Access places the words Database (Access 2002–2003 file format) in the title bar following the database name.

| Database (Access 2007) - Microsoft Access |

Access 2007 and 2010 file format title bar

| Database (Access 2002 - 2003 file format) - Microsoft Access |

Access 2002-2003 file format title bar

DEVELOP YOUR SKILLS 12.1.1
Save an Access 2010 Database in Access 2003 Format

In this exercise, you will save an existing Access 2010 database in a format recognized by Access 2003.

1. **Open** the iJams Original database from the Lesson 12 folder and **enable content**, if necessary.

2. Choose **File→Save & Publish→Save Database As→Access 2002–2003 Database** and then click the **Save As** button.

3. **Open** the folder in which you are storing your student files and type **iJams 2003** in the File Name textbox.
   Access opens the new database file and identifies the file format in the title bar as Access 2002–2003 file format.

4. **Close** the database.

12.2 Attaching Files to Database Records

Video Lesson   labyrinthelab.com/videos

As the number of records in each database table grows, the size of the database file grows, too. Database size has some effect on the speed and efficiency of the database. The more data you add to each record in a database, the larger the database becomes. To prevent adding repetitive data from files such as an Excel worksheet or a Word document in a comments or other memo field of a database record, many companies simply attach the file to the record. Attaching files to records prevents increasing the size of the database.

Using the Attachment Data Type

Access 2010 contains a data type that enables you to attach any file type to a database table record. You can use the Attachment data type when you want to attach pictures, spreadsheet files, documents, charts, and other file types to a specific field in the table—and store multiple files of varying file types together without increasing the size of the database file.

There are some basic guidelines that govern attaching files to database table records. These guidelines include the following:

Attachments are supported by

- Access 2007 and 2010 are the only versions of Access that allow you to attach files to database records.
- Access databases that contain attachments can only be viewed in Access 2007 or 2010 and are incompatible with previous versions of Access.
- Both the datasheet and design views enable you to assign the Attachment data type.

Attachment limitations

- A maximum limit of two gigabytes of data can be attached to a database.
- The file size for individual attachments is limited to 256 megabytes.
- After assigning the Attachment data type to a table field, you cannot change it.

Attachments are managed by

- The Attachments dialog box, which enables you to add, edit, and manage attachments.
- Opening attachment files, if the program used to create an attachment is installed on your computer.
- Saving attachments to local or network drives.

Managing Attachments

Access identifies fields that contain attachments with a paperclip icon in the field name and a paperclip icon followed by a number to identify the number of attachments for each individual record. To add an attachment, you double-click the icon for the record to which you want to attach the file. Access opens the Attachments dialog box, which makes managing attachments much easier.

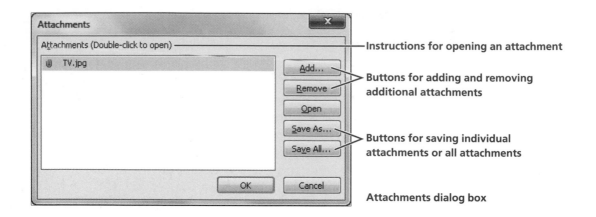

Instructions for opening an attachment

Buttons for adding and removing additional attachments

Buttons for saving individual attachments or all attachments

Attachments dialog box

QUICK REFERENCE	WORKING WITH ATTACHMENT FIELDS
Task	**Procedure**
Create an attachment field	▪ Display the table to contain the Attachment field in Design View. ▪ Type the new Field Name. ▪ Choose Attachment from the Data Type list. ▪ Save changes to the table.
Attach a file to a table record	▪ Display the table containing the Attachment field in Datasheet View. ▪ Double-click the paperclip icon for the record to which you want to attach a file to open the Attachment dialog box. ▪ Click the Add button and open the folder containing the file to attach. ▪ Double-click the filename to add it to the Attachment dialog box. ▪ Click OK.
Open a record attachment	▪ Open the table containing the record with the attachment. ▪ Double-click the paperclip icon for the record containing the attachment. ▪ Double-click the filename of the attachment to open. ▪ Close the attachment file and then click OK to close the Attachment dialog box.
Save a record attachment	▪ Open the table containing the record with the attachment. ▪ Double-click the paperclip icon for the record containing the attachment. ▪ Click the filename of the attachment to save and then click Save As. ▪ Save the item using standard save procedures. ▪ Click OK to close the Attachment dialog box.

Create an Attachment Field and Attach a File

In this exercise, you will add an Attachment field to the table Design View and attach a file to a table record.

1. **Open** the iJams Original database and **save** the file as a new database named **iJams MultiFormat**.

2. Display the iJams Inventory table in **Design View**.

3. Follow these steps to add a new field to the table:

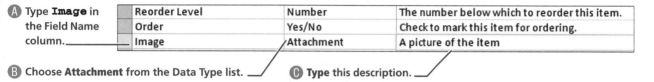

Ⓐ Type **Image** in the Field Name column.

Reorder Level	Number	The number below which to reorder this item.
Order	Yes/No	Check to mark this item for ordering.
Image	Attachment	A picture of the item

Ⓑ Choose **Attachment** from the Data Type list. Ⓒ **Type** this description.

4. **Save** 🖫 changes to the table and then display the table in **Datasheet View**.

5. Follow these steps to add an attachment to the first table record:

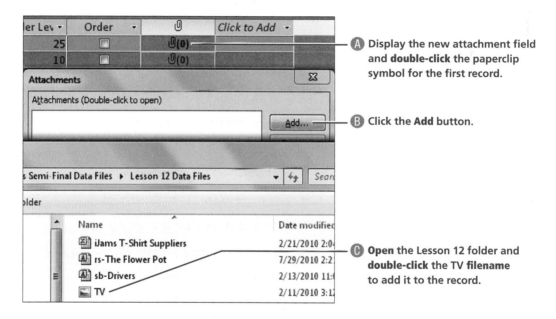

Ⓐ Display the new attachment field and **double-click** the paperclip symbol for the first record.

Ⓑ Click the **Add** button.

Ⓒ **Open** the Lesson 12 folder and **double-click** the TV **filename** to add it to the record.

Access adds the filename to the Attachments dialog box.

6. Choose **OK**.
   Access places the number 1 in parentheses following the attachment icon for record 1.

7. **Double-click** the paperclip icon for record 1 again to open the Attachments dialog box.

8. **Double-click** the attachment to open it.

9. **Close** the attachment window and then click **OK** to close the Attachments dialog box.

10. **Close** ☒ the table.

12.3 Integrating Access with Word

Video Lesson labyrinthelab.com/videos

Although there are any number of ways that you might want to share data between Access and Word, two prominent occasions come immediately to mind:

- Merging Access data records with a Word document.
- Publishing Access data in a Word document for inclusion in a report.

Export tools on the External Data tab of the Ribbon enable you to connect objects in a database to other Microsoft Office applications as well as to other file formats.

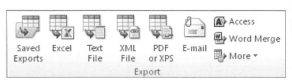

Export tools on the External Data tab of the Ribbon

QUICK REFERENCE	EXPORTING DATA TO WORD
Task	**Procedure**
Publish Access data with Word	• Open the table, form, or query results datasheet that you want to publish in Word. • Choose External Data→Export→Export to RTF on the Ribbon.
Merge data with Word	• Open the table or form containing the records you want to merge with Word. • Choose External Data→Export→More on the Ribbon. • Choose Merge It. • Select the option you want to use to select an existing merge document or to create a new one. • Use Word's Merge tools to complete the merge process.

Merging Access Data with Word Documents

Access databases often contain valuable data that would be appropriate to include in letters, mailings, and other documents. Retyping such data can be time-consuming and can also increase the potential for inaccurate data entry. When the data you want to use to create merge documents exists in Access, you will find the Access Export tool for merging data with Word a bonus.

When you use the Export tools to merge data with Word, Access gives you two options for using the data:

- **Link to an Existing Word Document:** Link the database table to an existing Word document so that Word then locates the database and pulls the data directly into the merge document. Linking the database to the document creates no new files to be maintained. However, the link that Access creates between the document and the database includes a path that is used to locate the data each time you open the merge document. If the database file is moved to a different folder, Word will be unable to locate it and you will have to establish the new path to the database to complete the merge.

- **Create a New Word Document:** Create a new Word document to merge with the data in the database table and link the new document to the Access database. The next time you open the Word document, Word automatically looks for the database containing the merge data.

Create a Merge Data Source Containing Access Data

In this exercise, you will export Access data and link it to a Word document.

Before You Begin: Your iJams MulitFormat database should be open.

1. Open the **iJams Customers** table.

2. Choose **External Data→Export→Word Merge** 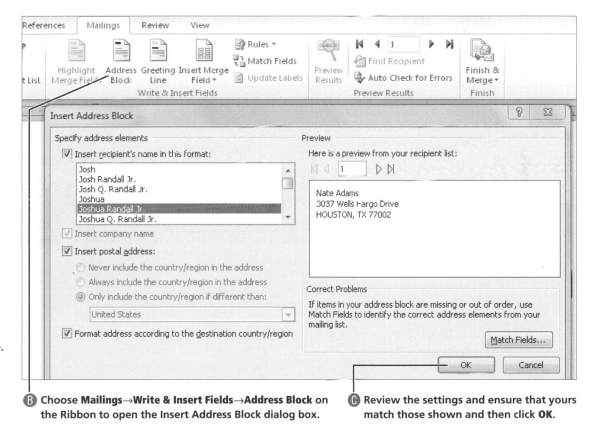.
   The Microsoft Word Mail Merge Wizard opens.

3. Choose the **Link Your Data to an Existing Microsoft Word Document** option and click **OK**.
   Access opens the Select Microsoft Word Document dialog box.

4. **Open** the Lesson 12 folder and **double-click** the iJams Product Offerings document to open it.
   Word launches and opens the document you selected along with the Mail Merge task pane.

5. Close the **Mail Merge** task pane and then follow these steps to add fields to the merge document:

Ⓐ Position the **insertion point** at the beginning of the line Insert Fields from Access database here.

Ⓑ Choose **Mailings→Write & Insert Fields→Address Block** on the Ribbon to open the Insert Address Block dialog box.

Ⓒ Review the settings and ensure that yours match those shown and then click **OK**.

6. **Delete** the text *Insert Fields from Access database here.*

7. Choose **Mailings→Preview Results→Preview Results** on the Ribbon to ensure that the data formats properly.

8. **Save** 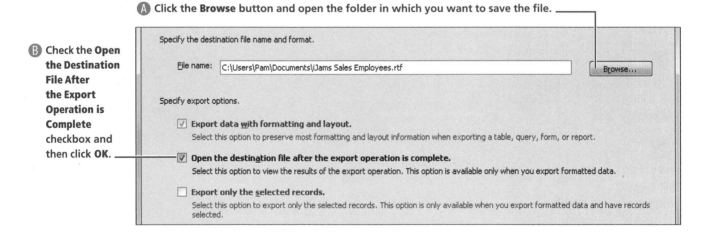 and **close** ☒ the document.

9. Switch back to **Access** and then **close** the iJams Customers table.

Publishing Data to Word

Video Lesson   labyrinthelab.com/videos

The most commonly used tools for integrating Access data with other applications appear directly on the Export group of the External Data tab of the Ribbon as the Word Merge tool did. Other tools appear on the More list of the External Data→Export group. These tools enable you to send data from a database object to Word. When you export a database object to Word, Access formats it in rich text format, launches Word, and opens the data in a new document. You can then edit the document in Word and save the file using the filename you choose—*without affecting the data in the database*.

DEVELOP YOUR SKILLS 12.3.2
Send Access Data to Word

In this exercise, you will export a list of iJams' sales employees to Word.

Before You Begin: Your iJams MultiFormat database should be open.

1. Open the **iJams Sales Employees** table.

2. Choose the **External Data→Export→More** menu and select **Word**.

3. Follow these steps to export the table to Word:

Ⓐ Click the **Browse** button and open the folder in which you want to save the file.

Ⓑ Check the **Open the Destination File After the Export Operation is Complete** checkbox and then click **OK**.

Specify the destination file name and format.

File name: C:\Users\Pam\Documents\iJams Sales Employees.rtf   Browse...

Specify export options.

☑ **Export data with formatting and layout.**
Select this option to preserve most formatting and layout information when exporting a table, query, form, or report.

☑ **Open the destination file after the export operation is complete.**
Select this option to view the results of the export operation. This option is available only when you export formatted data.

☐ **Export only the selected records.**
Select this option to export only the selected records. This option is only available when you export formatted data and have records selected.

Access exports the table and opens it in Word.

4. Close the **Export – RTF File** dialog box and switch to **Word**.

5. Choose **Page Layout→Page Setup→Orientation** 🖼 on the Ribbon, and then choose **Landscape** to fit the data horizontally on the page.

6. **Close** the file, **saving** changes when prompted, and then switch back to **Access**.

7. **Close** ☒ the table.

Copying Data from Access to Word

Video Lesson labyrinthelab.com/videos

In addition to the special tools Access provides for sharing data with Word, there are also techniques for copying data from Access tables into Word. These techniques can be useful when you want to share only a portion of data contained in a table with a Word file or when you want to place a copy of a database object such as a form or report in a Word document.

You can use both copy-and-paste and drag-and-drop techniques to copy Access data into a Word document. Remember, though, that editing the copied data has no effect on the data stored in the database—you are copying data that represents a specific date and time, and the data may be out of date as the database records change.

DEVELOP YOUR SKILLS 12.3.3
Copy Data from Access to a Word Document

In this exercise, you will copy data from an Access table into a new Word document using both the copy-and-paste and drag-and-drop techniques.

Before You Begin: Your iJams MultiFormat database should be open.

1. Open the **iJams Inventory** table and sort the table in **ascending** order on the **Category** field.

2. **Scroll down** the table until the TV category is visible and then follow these steps to copy all records for TVs:

Ⓐ Click the **record selector button** for the first record in the TV category and drag the down the selector buttons to select all TV records.

Ⓑ Choose **Home→ Clipboard→ Copy** on the Ribbon.

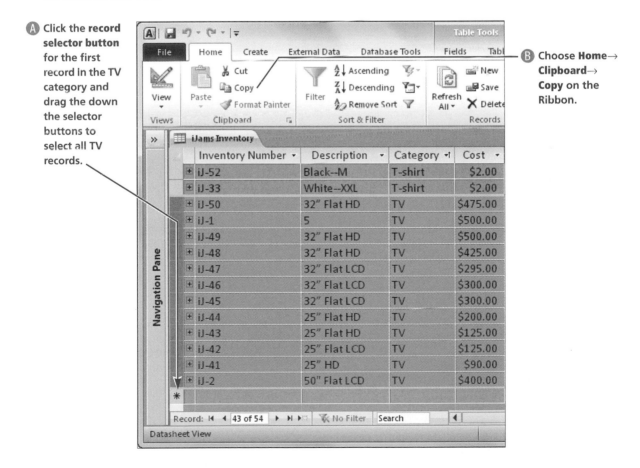

Inventory Number	Description	Category	Cost
iJ-52	Black--M	T-shirt	$2.00
iJ-33	White--XXL	T-shirt	$2.00
iJ-50	32" Flat HD	TV	$475.00
iJ-1	5	TV	$500.00
iJ-49	32" Flat HD	TV	$500.00
iJ-48	32" Flat HD	TV	$425.00
iJ-47	32" Flat LCD	TV	$295.00
iJ-46	32" Flat LCD	TV	$300.00
iJ-45	32" Flat LCD	TV	$300.00
iJ-44	25" Flat HD	TV	$200.00
iJ-43	25" Flat HD	TV	$125.00
iJ-42	25" Flat LCD	TV	$125.00
iJ-41	25" HD	TV	$90.00
iJ-2	50" Flat LCD	TV	$400.00

Record: 43 of 54   No Filter   Search

Datasheet View

3. Launch **Word** (or switch to Word) and create a new blank document.

4. Choose **Home→Clipboard→Paste** to paste the data from the 12 records into the document; then **press** ⌕Enter⌕ twice.

5. **Minimize** all applications and then maximize Word and Access.

6. Follow these steps to arrange Word and Access onscreen:

Ⓐ **Right-click** a blank area of the task bar.

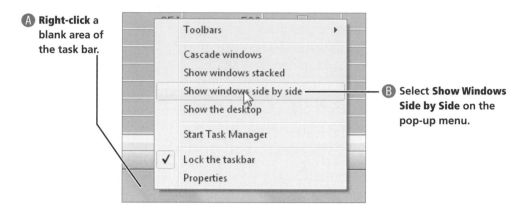

Ⓑ Select **Show Windows Side by Side** on the pop-up menu.

Access arranges all maximized application windows side by side within the computer window.

7. Follow these steps to drag the selected records to the Word document:

Ⓐ Select all four **MP3 Player** records in Access.

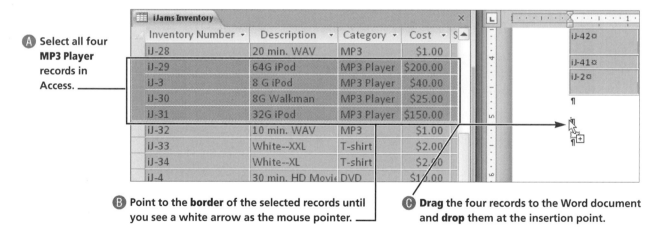

Ⓑ Point to the **border** of the selected records until you see a white arrow as the mouse pointer.

Ⓒ **Drag** the four records to the Word document and **drop** them at the insertion point.

8. **Save** 💾 the Word document using the filename **Access Data**; then **close** the document, **exit** Word, and **maximize** Access.

You can use these same techniques to drag Access table data into Excel or PowerPoint, too!

12.4 Integrating Access with Excel

Video Lesson labyrinthelab.com/videos

Sharing data between two Microsoft Office application involves more than just exporting Access data to Word. It also involves importing data from other applications. In this section, you will explore both importing and exporting data between Access and Excel.

Importing Data from Excel Files

Many people consider the calculation capabilities in Excel more sophisticated than those available in Access. They also find the formulas easier to create in Excel than calculated fields in Access. As a result, Access data is often used in Excel to perform calculations, with the data being imported into Access after the calculations are complete. This process of retrieving data from other files is called *importing* data.

When you import data from other programs, Access examines the file and prompts you for information about the file so that data is imported accurately. In the case of an Excel worksheet, Access uses the Import Spreadsheet Wizard to guide the process. After you import the data, it becomes part of the database file. Changes you make to the Excel file have no impact on the table data in Access.

Tools on the External Data tab of the Ribbon are used to import as well as export data. The group containing the tool controls whether you retrieve data from Excel into Access or whether you send Access data to Excel:

Excel tool for importing is on the Import & Link group.

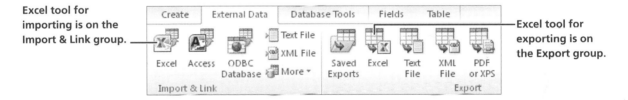

Excel tool for exporting is on the Export group.

QUICK REFERENCE	IMPORTING AND EXPORTING EXCEL FILES
Task	**Procedure**
Import data from Excel	■ Choose External Data→Import & Link→Excel on the Ribbon. ■ Navigate to the folder containing the file you want to import and open the folder. ■ Double-click the filename of the file you want to import.
Export Access data to Excel	■ Select or open the database object you want to export to Excel. ■ Choose External Data→Export→Excel on the Ribbon ■ Navigate to the folder into which you want to save the new Excel file and select appropriate options. ■ Click OK.

Import Excel Data into Access

In this exercise, you will import an Excel worksheet containing a list of T-shirt suppliers into the iJams MultiFormat database.

Before you begin: Your iJams MultiFormat database should be open.

1. **Close** all Access database objects and choose **External Data→Import & Link→ Excel** on the Ribbon.
   Access launches the Get External Data – Excel Spreadsheet dialog box.

2. Click the **Browse** button and navigate to the Lesson 12 folder containing your student data files.

3. **Double-click** the iJams T-shirt Suppliers.xlsx **filename** to open the file.

4. Select the **Import the Source Data into a New Table in the Current Database** option and click **OK** to launch the Import Spreadsheet Wizard.

5. Select the **Show Worksheets** option and then click **Next** to display the second Wizard screen.

6. Check the **First Row Contains Column Headings** checkbox and then click **Next**.

7. Click **Next** to indicate that all fields in the worksheet should import to the new table.

8. Click **Next** to let Access create a Primary Key.

9. Click **Next** and type `iJams T-shirt Suppliers` in the Import to Table field and click **Finish**.

10. Choose **Close** to close the Get External Data window.

View Data

11. Open the new **iJams T-shirt Suppliers** table to view the data.

12. Adjust column widths, **save** changes to the table, and **close** it.

Exporting Access Data to Excel

Video Lesson	labyrinthelab.com/videos

When you want to use Excel to work with the data, you can export the Access data to create a new Excel file. After exporting the file from Access to Excel, you often have some cleanup work to complete the worksheet format. For example, when values in an Access table are formatted as Text data types, Excel reports an error for the data that you can correct. In addition, Excel formats AutoNumber values as text and reports an error. You can correct each of these errors and then create formulas or add other columns to finish the worksheet.

The procedures used to export a file to Excel are similar to the procedures used to export Access data to merge with Word.

Export Access Data to Create a New Excel Workbook

In this exercise, you will export data from the Inventory table to create a new Excel workbook.

Before You Begin: Your iJams MulitFormat database should be open.

1. Click the **iJams Inventory** table in the Navigation Pane to select it.

2. Choose **External Data→Export→Export to Excel Spreadsheet** [icon] on the Ribbon to open the Export – Excel Spreadsheet dialog box.

3. Click the **Browse** button and **open** the folder into which you want to save the new workbook.

4. Ensure that the File Format is set to **Excel Workbook (*.xlsx)** and check the **Export Data with Formatting** and **Layout and Open the Destination File When the Export Operation is Complete** checkboxes.

5. Click **OK** to save the file and then click **Close** to close the Export dialog box.
   Excel opens and displays the new workbook containing the inventory data. Your worksheet should resemble the one shown in the following illustration.

The Image column shows the number of attachments present for each record.

Triangles identify error messages related to Input Mask settings in Access.

	A	B	C	D	E	F	G	H	I
1	Inventory Number	Description	Category	Cost	Sales Price	Quantity in Stock	Reorder Level	Order	Image
2	iJ-1	50"	TV	$500.00	$2,000.00	20	25	FALSE	1
3	iJ-10	5-Disk HD Player	DVD Player	$300.00	$450.00	10	10	FALSE	0
4	iJ-11	10-Disk Player	DVD Player	$375.00	$600.00	8	10	FALSE	0
5		20"	Monitor	$200.00	$300.00	5	5	FALSE	0
6	iJ-13	20"	Monitor	$175.00	$300.00	6	5	FALSE	0
7	iJ-14	24"	Monitor	$225.00	$400.00	10	5	FALSE	0
8	iJ-15	27"	Monitor	$325.00	$500.00	8	5	FALSE	0

iJams Inventory

The table name appears as the sheet name.

6. **Close** [X] the workbook, **exit** Excel, and **switch back** to Access.

Linking an Excel Worksheet to an Access Database

Video Lesson   labyrinthelab.com/videos

Earlier in this lesson, you imported Excel data to create a new table. Each time you import data from Excel to Access, the data you import contains fixed values found in the spreadsheet at the time you import. When you want the data in the Access database to reflect the most current data contained in the Excel spreadsheet, you can import and link the Excel spreadsheet to the Access database table. When you link a spreadsheet to a database, each time you make a change to the data in Excel, the change is reflected in Access when you open the linked spreadsheet table in Access. Access identifies linked spreadsheets using the Excel icon that displays an arrow to show that it is linked to the original Excel spreadsheet, as shown here. No edits can be made to the spreadsheet from within the Access table.

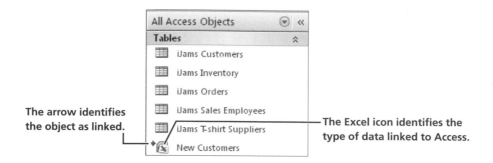

The arrow identifies the object as linked.

The Excel icon identifies the type of data linked to Access.

Link an Excel Spreadsheet to an Access Database

In this exercise, you will link a spreadsheet containing a new list of customers to the iJams database.

Before You Begin: Your iJams MulitFormat database should be open.

1. Choose **External Data→Import & Link→Excel** on the Ribbon to open the Get External Data—Excel Spreadsheet dialog box.

2. Choose the **Link to the Data Source by Creating a Linked Table** option and then click the **Browse** button and open the Lesson 12 folder.

3. **Double-click** the file Customer Data.xlsx to open it and then choose **OK** to launch the Link Spreadsheet Wizard.

4. Click **Next** to accept Sheet1 from the first wizard screen.

5. Check the **First Row Contains Column Headings** checkbox and then click **Next**.

6. Type **New Customers** in the Linked Table Name text box and click **Finish**.

7. Click **OK** to acknowledge the Link Spreadsheet Wizard message and locate the linked item as identified by the Excel icon and arrow in the Tables list.

8. Open the **linked spreadsheet** in Access and try to edit the data.
   Access prevents data editing when the linked file is open in Access.

9. **Close** X the datasheet.

Fixing Broken Links

Video Lesson labyrinthelab.com/videos

When you link an Excel spreadsheet to an Access database, Access identifies the drive and folder in which the Excel file was located at the time you created the link. Access searches for the Excel file each time you open the database. As files move to new folders and onto removable disks and drives for travel, the path is often no longer valid and Access is unable to locate or connect to the linked file. As a result, Access contains a feature called the Linked Table Manager that aids in locating and redirecting the database to the correct file so that you can view the data.

The file linked to the database and the folder and drive in which it is stored. ———

Checking this checkbox tells Access to open the Select New Location dialog box so you can redirect the link to a moved file. ———

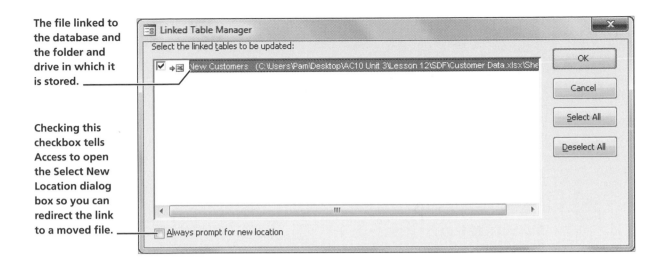

DEVELOP YOUR SKILLS 12.4.4

Use the Linked Table Manager

In this exercise, you will open the Linked Table Manager and view the linked file.

Before You Begin: Your iJams MulitFormat database should be open.

1. Choose **External Data→Import & Link→Linked Table Manager** on the Ribbon to open the Linked Table Manager dialog box.

2. Follow these steps to review the information contained in the dialog box:

Ⓐ **Click** the checkbox beside the linked **filename** and review the linked file identified. ———

Ⓑ Check the **Always Prompt for New Location** checkbox. ———

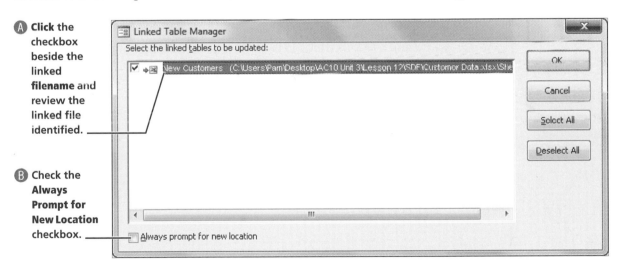

3. Choose **OK**.
   Because you set the Always Prompt for New Location option, Access displays a dialog box to enable you to navigate to the folder containing the file.

4. Locate the Customer Data.xlsx file and choose **Open**.

5. Click **OK** and then click **Close**.

12.5 Collecting Data Using Outlook

Video Lesson   labyrinthelab.com/videos

A feature that premiered in Access 2007—*data collection*—works with Outlook 2010 to collect data from people throughout the world. From Access, you can generate an email message that contains a data entry form. The recipients then complete the form and send them back to you. After all the replies are received, you process the responses.

Data collection can be used to distribute many types of information-gathering forms, such as:

- Surveys
- Status Reports
- New Customer Information Forms
- New Inventory Item Forms

Setting Up to Collect Data

Before using the data collection feature, you first need to ensure that the appropriate tools are available. Ensure that:

- Microsoft Office Access 2010 and Outlook 2010 are installed and running properly on your computer.
- Recipients have an email program that supports HTML format.
- A database is identified into which you want to gather the data—the destination database.
- Tables are set up and available to hold the returned data.
- You have determined whether the data will create new records or update existing records.

Sending a Request for Data

As with many other features in Access 2010, a wizard is available to help set up data collection. When you launch the data collection process, Access presents the following screen that outlines the steps you will go through to complete the request:

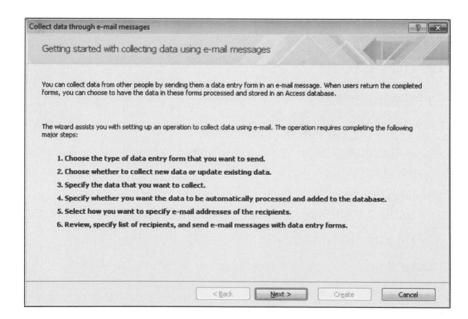

As you work through the wizard screens, you are asked to determine each of the following:

- **Form Type:** Identify the type of form you want to attach—HTML or InfoPath. HTML forms require fewer software restrictions and are universally more available to recipients.

- **Data Handling:** Specify what you want to do with the data after it is returned: add the data as new records or update existing records.

- **Fields Required:** Select the fields to include on the form. Remember that the primary and foreign key fields must contain data, so they must be included on the form.

- **Data Processing:** Determine how to process the data. You can process the data automatically or manually. If you choose automatic processing, Outlook and Access work together to export the form of each reply to the appropriate table in the destination database. If you choose manual processing, you simply choose the replies you want to export to Access when the response arrives in Outlook. No data entry is required.

- **Processing Options:** Set additional processing options. On this screen, you choose the name of the Outlook folder into which you want the responses gathered. In addition, you can choose options that control whether multiple responses from each recipient are allowed, how many responses to process, and a cutoff date for processing replies.

- **Select Recipients:** Identify the procedure you want to use to specify email addresses of recipients: type the email addresses or add a field to the table set up to collect the data.

- **Complete the Message:** Type and send the email message to accompany the form.

QUICK REFERENCE	USING DATA COLLECTION TOOLS
Task	**Procedure**
Send a form for data collection	■ Open the destination database containing the table into which you want the collected data to appear.
	■ Select the table in the Navigation Pane.
	■ Choose External Data→Collect Data→Create E-mail on the Ribbon and follow the wizard steps to create and send the email message.
View responses	■ Switch to Outlook 2010.
	■ Open the folder you specified to collect the responses.
	■ Open the message and review the form.

DEVELOP YOUR SKILLS 12.5.1
Send Requests for Data

WebSim   labyrinthelab.com/acc10

In this exercise, you will send an email message from Access 2010 to a recipient for data collection.

1. **Type** the URL for the student web page (listed above) in the address bar of your web browser and **tap** [Enter].

2. From the left navigation bar, click **Lessons 9–12** and then **Lesson 12**; then click the **Develop Your Skills 12.5.1 Send Requests for Data** link.

3. Work your way through the **on-screen exercise instructions**.

4. Click the **Back to Course** link at the top-right corner of your screen.

Managing Replies

Video Lesson   labyrinthelab.com/videos

Now that you have sent the message, recipients should receive it in their inboxes. When they complete the form, all they have to do is click Reply, complete the form, and then click the Send button. Because you selected the option to automatically process responses, Outlook will collect the responses and send them on to Access, placing them into the table you specified when you sent the message—in this case, the iJams Customers table. You will also be able to view the responses from the folder in Outlook.

DEVELOP YOUR SKILLS 12.5.2

Manage Replies

WebSim   labyrinthelab.com/acc10

In this exercise, you will open the request for data you sent in the last activity and reply with a completed form. In addition, you will also view the reply message in Outlook as well as in Access.

1. If necessary, **type** the URL listed above in the address bar of your web browser and **tap** Enter.

2. From the left navigation bar, click **Lessons 9–12** and then **Lesson 12**; then click the **Develop Your Skills 12.5.2 Manage Replies** link.

3. Work your way through the **on-screen exercise instructions**.

4. Click the **Back to Course** link at the top-right corner of your screen.

12.6 Displaying Access Data on the Web

Video Lesson   labyrinthelab.com/videos

In addition to sharing data from Access with other Microsoft Office applications, you can also save database objects in formats for other uses and import data from other formats. For example, when you want to store Access data on the web, you could save the data in HTML format. In addition, there may be times when you want to add web page access to database objects. You can add a hyperlink to the object that automatically opens the web page from Access.

Exporting Access Objects as Web Pages

Hypertext Markup Language (HTML) contains coding to format a document for viewing in a web browser. When a database object is saved in HTML format, anyone who has access to the file can view the data using Internet Explorer or another web browser such as Firefox. You can save each database object separately as an HTML document. HTML documents display data from database tables at a specific point in time.

Updating HTML Data

When data in the database changes, HTML documents do not automatically update to reflect those changes. Many companies update their HTML files regularly, and display a date and time to indicate when the data was current. To create an HTML file for a database object, you export the object.

Saving HTML Formatted Objects

The Export data with formatting and layout option appears in the Export dialog box when you export a document to HTML format. By default, the option is checked to enable you to preserve formatting that is active when you export a form. When you export other database objects, such as tables, you have the choice to export with formatting or not. When you click OK, Access displays the HTML Output Options dialog box so you can choose a template or an encoding to apply to the file. The encoding Access applies to HTML files simply formats it for use on the web.

Setting Export Options

When you export tables to create HTML files, Access presents the HTML Output Options dialog box so you can select an HTML template or code the data. You want to assign the default encoding, so no other actions are required.

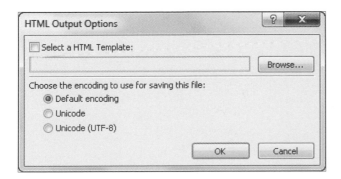

IMPORTING AND EXPORTING DATABASE OBJECTS AS HTML FILES

Task	Procedure
Export a database object in HTML format	■ Select the object to export. ■ Choose External Data→Export→More →HTML Document ▦ on the Ribbon. ■ Click Browse and open the folder in which you want to save the file. ■ Choose Open the Destination File After the Export Operation is Complete. (Optional) ■ Click OK.
View HTML data in a web browser	■ Launch your web browser. ■ Choose File→Open and locate the file to open. ■ Double-click the filename to open it.
Import HTML data	■ Open the database into which you want to import HTML data. ■ Choose External Data→Import→More →HTML Document ▦ on the Ribbon. ■ Click Browse and open the folder containing the file to import. ■ Double-click the file to open it and select the import, append, or link option listed. ■ Click OK and work through each wizard screen, selecting appropriate options and clicking Next to advance to the next screen. ■ Click Finish.

DEVELOP YOUR SKILLS 12.6.1

Export a Table in HTML Format

In this exercise, you will export a form in HTML format and view it in a web browser.

Before You Begin: Your iJams MulitFormat database should be open.

1. Click the **iJams Customer Orders** form to select it (but do not open it).

2. Choose **External Data→Export→More→HTML Document** ▦ on the Ribbon.

3. Click **Browse, open** the folder containing your student data files, and click **Save**.

4. Place a checkmark in the **Open the Destination File After the Export Operation Is Complete** option box.

5. Click **OK**.
   Access opens the HTML Output Options dialog box.

6. Click **OK** to create the file without changing the default settings.
   Access creates the HTML file and opens the file in your default web browser.

7. Switch back to **Access** and then click **Close** to close the dialog box.

Importing HTML Files

Video Lesson   labyrinthelab.com/videos

When data you want to use in an Access database already exists in an HTML document, you can import the data to create a new table in a database or to append an existing table. In addition, you can link the HTML file to the database. The procedures for importing HTML data are similar to those used to import Excel and other types of data.

DEVELOP YOUR SKILLS 12.6.2

Import an HTML File as a Database Object

In this exercise, you will import a new list of inventory items contained in an HTML file into Access as a new table.

Before You Begin: Your iJams MulitFormat database should be open.

1. **Close** all open database objects.

2. Choose **External Data→Import→More→HTML Document** 🔲 on the Ribbon.

3. Click **Browse** and **open** the Lesson 12 folder.

4. **Double-click** the iJams Inventory 2010 file to open it and select the **Import the Source Data into a New Table in the Current Database** option.

5. Click **OK** to launch the Import HTML Wizard.

6. Work through each wizard screen, selecting the following options and clicking **Next** to advance to the next screen:

   ■ Screen 1: Check the **First Row Contains Column Headings** checkbox.

   ■ Screen 2: Accept default settings by just clicking **Next**.

   ■ Screen 3: Select **Choose My Own Primary Key** option and ensure that **Inventory Number** is displayed in the option text box.

   ■ Screen 4: Click **Finish**.

7. Click **Close** to close the Get External Data dialog box and then **open** the iJams Inventory 2010 table.

8. Review the data and then **close** ☒ the table.

Adding Hyperlinks to Database Objects

Video Lesson labyrinthelab.com/videos

Hyperlinks attached to database forms and reports provide a convenient way to access other objects in the database, external files associated with the database, or websites. Users can click the hyperlink to access the file or object associated with the hyperlink.

You can create a hyperlink to serve purposes such as:

■ Creating a new table field, formatting it as a hyperlink data type, and entering a customer's email address

■ Adding the hyperlink field to a form so that you can send a quick email each time a customer places an order

■ Adding a hyperlink to a report that opens a website that is related to the company or database in the report

■ Adding a hyperlink to a form that launches another application and opens a file

Options in the Insert Hyperlink dialog box enable you to select an existing file or web page, an object in the active database, or an email address. Although the hyperlink text generally identifies the action of the hyperlink, you can add a ScreenTip to display when the user points to the hyperlink.

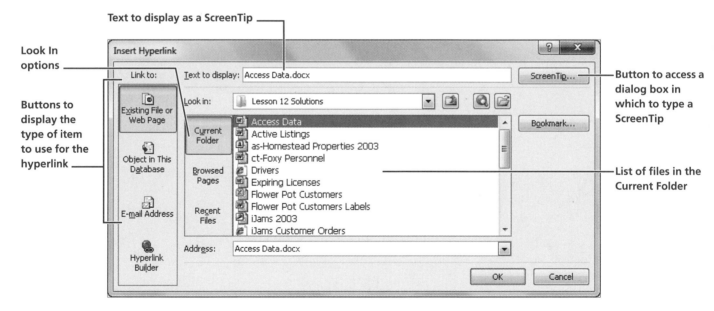

Using Hyperlinks

Normally, hyperlinks are formatted using a different color text and are sometimes underlined. Regardless of how the hyperlink text is formatted, when you point to the text or object that contains a hyperlink, the mouse pointer appears as a pointing hand. Clicking (rather than double-clicking) performs the action associated with the hyperlink.

QUICK REFERENCE	INSERTING, EDITING, AND REMOVING A HYPERLINK ON A DATABASE OBJECT
Task	**Procedure**
Add a hyperlink as an object	■ Display the object in Design View. ■ Choose Design→Controls→Insert Hyperlink 🌐 on the Ribbon to open the Insert Hyperlink dialog box. ■ Locate the file or website to which you want to link. ■ Add ScreenTip Text to Display. (Optional) ■ Click OK.
Edit hyperlink	■ Open the object containing the hyperlink in Design View. ■ Right-click the hyperlink control and choose Hyperlink→Edit Hyperlink to open the Edit Hyperlink dialog box. ■ Make the necessary edits in the Edit Hyperlink dialog box and click OK.
Remove hyperlink	■ Open the object containing the hyperlink in Design View. ■ Right-click the hyperlink control and choose Hyperlink→Remove Hyperlink.
Delete hyperlink	■ Open the object containing the hyperlink in Design View. ■ Right-click the hyperlink control and choose Delete. *or* ■ Click the control to select the hyperlink and press Delete.

Add a Hyperlink to a Database Form

In this exercise, you will add a hyperlink to the iJams Customer Orders form that displays the iJams Inventory datasheet.

Before You Begin: Your iJams MulitFormat database should be open.

1. Open the iJams Customer Orders form in **Design View**.

2. Choose **Design→Controls→Insert Hyperlink** 🌐 on the Ribbon to open the Insert Hyperlink dialog box.

3. Follow these steps to add a hyperlink to the form that opens a table:

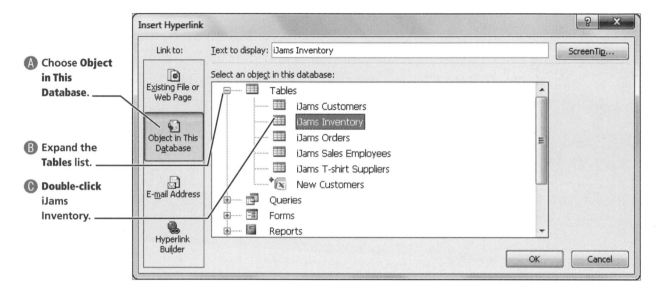

A Choose **Object in This Database**.

B Expand the **Tables** list.

C **Double-click** iJams Inventory.

Access places the hyperlink control in the upper-left corner of the form Detail section.

4. **Drag** the control to about the **4"** mark on the vertical ruler and about the **1/2"** mark on the horizontal ruler.

5. **Save** 💾 changes to the form and then switch to **Form View**.

6. Click the **iJams Inventory** hyperlink to open the table.

7. **Close** all database objects.

12.7 Concepts Review

Concepts Review   labyrinthelab.com/acc10

To check your knowledge of the key concepts introduced in this lesson, complete the Concepts Review quiz by going to the URL listed above. If your classroom is using Labyrinth eLab, you may complete the Concepts Review quiz from within your eLab course.

Reinforce Your Skills

REINFORCE YOUR SKILLS 12.1

Export Table Data to Excel

The versatility of 256 columns and over 65,500 rows available in each Excel spreadsheet makes it a logical application to hold data from a database—especially when the database contains large volumes of data. Excel also contains tools that you can use to analyze data. As a result, The Flower Pot chose to export data from its Access database to Excel. In this exercise, you will export data from the rs-Flower Pot MultiFormat database to an Excel file.

1. **Open** the rs-Flower Pot MultiFormat database from the Lesson 12 folder and display the **Navigation Pane**.

2. Select the **Flower Pot Customers** table.

3. Choose **External Data→Export→Export to Excel Spreadsheet** 📑 on the Ribbon.

4. Click the **Browse** button and **open** the folder in which you are saving your student files.

5. Click **Save** and then check the **Export Data with Formatting and Layout** checkbox.

6. Check the **Open the Destination File After the Export Operation is Complete** checkbox.

7. Click **OK**.

8. Review the data in the Excel spreadsheet and then exit **Excel**.

9. Switch back to **Access** and then **close** the dialog box.

REINFORCE YOUR SKILLS 12.2

Publish a Report in Word

The rs-Flower Pot MultiFormat database contains a report that prints labels. In this exercise, you will publish the labels report in Word.

Before You Begin: Your rs-Flower Pot MultiFormat database should be open.

1. Open the **Flower Pot Customers Labels** report.

2. Choose **External Data→Export→More→Word** 📑 on the Ribbon.

3. Click the **Browse** button and **open** the folder in which you are storing your student files.

4. Choose **Save** and then check the **Open the Destination File After the Export Operation Is Complete** checkbox.

5. Click **OK**.
   Access sends the labels report to Word and opens the new file in Word.

6. Review the labels, exit **Word**, and return to **Access**.

7. Click **Close** to close the dialog box.

8. **Close** the database.

Merge Records with a Word File

Each year, the drivers licensing bureau in each state must submit a list of drivers whose licenses expire that year to insurance companies. The rs-Drivers database in your Lesson 12 folder contains a query that displays the expiration date for each license. In this exercise, you will use the query to generate the report by merging records from the query with Word to create a table.

1. **Open** the rs-Drivers database, **save** the database as a new file named **rs-Drivers Web**, and then **open** the License Expires query to review data.

2. Choose **External Data→Export→Word Merge** 📄 on the Ribbon.

3. Choose the **Create a New Document and Then Link the Data to It** option.

4. Click **OK** to launch Word and display a new document with the Mailings tools displayed on the Ribbon.

5. Close the **Mail Merge** task pane.

6. Choose **Mailings→Start Mail Merge→Edit Recipient List** 📋 on the Ribbon to open the Mail Merge Recipients list.

7. Follow these steps to set up a filter for choosing recipients:

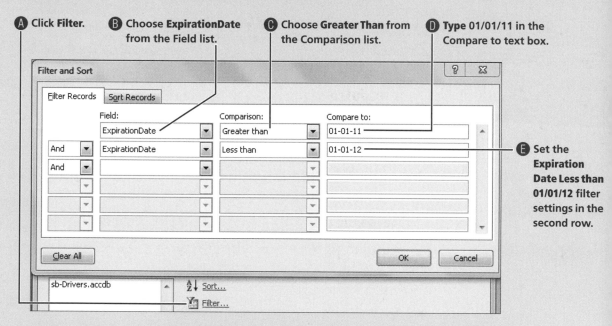

Ⓐ **Click Filter.** Ⓑ **Choose ExpirationDate from the Field list.** Ⓒ **Choose Greater Than from the Comparison list.** Ⓓ **Type 01/01/11 in the Compare to text box.**

Ⓔ **Set the Expiration Date Less than 01/01/12 filter settings in the second row.**

8. Click **OK** to close both dialog boxes, and then choose **Mailings→Write & Insert Fields→Insert Merge Field** on the Ribbon to open the Insert Merge Field dialog box.

9. **Double-click** each of the following fields to add the field to the document: DriverID, FirstName, LastName, ExpirationDate, and AutoInsurance.

10. Close the **Insert Merge Field** dialog box and **add** spacing between double chevrons
    (<< >>) to separate the fields and create the layout shown in the following illustration:

<<DriverID>> <<FirstName>> <<LastName>>
<<ExpirationDate>> <<AutoInsurance>>

11. Choose **Mailings→Preview Results→Preview Results** on the Ribbon to display
    the record.

12. **Save** the document using the filename **Expiring Licenses**.

13. **Print** a copy of the document, **close** the file, and then **exit** Word.

14. Switch to **Access** and **close** the query.

REINFORCE YOUR SKILLS 12.4

Add a Hyperlink to a Database Form

*The Drivers database is being developed for distribution to many states. Eventually, it will be formatted so
that the data can be posted on a secure site on the web so that each state will be able to link to records from
other states and access driver data. Before formatting the page for the web, the form needs to contain a
hyperlink that opens the Drivers table. In this exercise, you will add a hyperlink to a form in the database.*

Before You Begin: Your rs-Drivers Web database should be open.

1. Display **All Access Objects** in the Navigation Pane and then open the **Drivers** form in
   Design View.

2. Choose **Design→Controls→Insert Hyperlink** on the Ribbon.

3. Click **Object in This Database** in the Link to bar, expand the **Tables** list, and select the
   Drivers table.

4. Click the **Text to Display** box, type **Open Drivers Table**, and click **OK**.

5. Drag the **hyperlink** so that it appears below the Restrictions control text box on the form.

6. **Save** changes to the form and then switch to **Form View**.

7. Click the **hyperlink** to ensure that it opens the correct object and then **close** all
   database objects.

Save a Form in HTML Format

Posting files on the web so representatives can access them is important to most states. However, the format used to export database objects determines whether hyperlinks contained on forms and reports work when you export them from Access. To show representatives from different states how easy it is to format data for the web, they have asked you to demonstrate. In this exercise, you will export a form that contains a hyperlink to create a web page and then test the hyperlink by viewing the web page in a browser to see if the hyperlink accesses the database object.

Before You Begin: Your rs-Drivers Web database should be open.

1. **Right-click** the Drivers form and choose **Export→HTML Document**.

2. Click the **Browse** button and **open** the folder in which you are storing your student files.

3. Click **Save** and then check the **Open the Destination File After the Export Operation Is Complete** checkbox.

4. Click **OK** and then click **OK** again to accept the default HTML Output Options.

5. Review the page and notice that the data exported to the HTML file as a table.

6. **Print** a copy of the page and then **exit** the browser.

7. Switch to **Access** and **close** the dialog box.

Send a Request for Data and Process the Reply

WebSim   labyrinthelab.com/acc10

In this exercise, you will send a request for data to your email address to obtain data for the Drivers table in the database. In addition, you will process the data automatically to append the table.

1. If necessary, **type** the URL listed above into the address bar of your web browser and tap Enter.

2. From the left navigation bar, click **Lessons 9–12** and then **Lesson 12**; then click the **Reinforce Your Skills 12.6 Send a Request for Data and Process the Reply** link.

3. Work your way through the **on-screen exercise instructions**.

4. Click the **Back to Course** link at the top-right corner of your screen.

Apply Your Skills

Save an Access Database in Access 2003 Format and Export Data to Excel

Homestead Properties plans to make their database accessible to users who have Access 2003 installed rather than Access 2010. Before completing the database, they want to ensure that all objects in the database are accessible to their users. In this exercise, you will save the database in a format accessible from Access 2003 and then export table data to Excel.

1. **Open** the as-Homestead database from the Lesson 12 folder.

2. **Save** the file as an Access 2002-2003 Database using the filename **as-Homestead Properties 2003**.

3. Open the **Properties** table and export the table data to an **Excel worksheet** using the default filename and ensure that formatting and layout is included.

4. **Open** the spreadsheet, **widen** the columns to display data, and **print** a copy of the data.

5. **Close** the file and **exit** Excel.

6. **Close** all database objects.

Add Hyperlinks to a Form

Clients of Homestead Properties frequently find homes listed by other realty companies in the area and call their realtor at Homestead Properties to find out more information about the properties. One way that Homestead Properties personnel have discovered can provide the most up-to-date information about other company listings is by connecting to their sites online. In this exercise, you will add a form to the as-Homestead Properties 2003 database that contains links to the most frequently visited realty company sites.

Before You Begin: Your as-Homestead Properties 2003 database should be open.

1. Open the Locate a Property form in **Design View**.

2. Add a **hyperlink control** to the Detail area of the form that links to an Existing File or Web Page.

3. Complete the following details in the Insert Hyperlink dialog box:
   - Type **www.century21.com** in the Address text box.
   - Type **Century21** in the Text to Display text box.

4. Repeat the procedures outlined in **step 3 to** add the following additional links to the form:

Website Address	Text to Dispay
www.remax.com	REMAX
www.coldwellbanker.com	Coldwell Banker
www.betterhomesrealty.com	Better Homes Realty

5. Format the controls so that the hyperlink text is larger, size the controls to accommodate the text, and position the controls evenly in the Detail section of the form.

6. **Save** 💾 the form and then display it in **Form View** to test each hyperlink. **Close** each web page before accessing the next one.

7. **Print** a copy of the form and then **close** ✕ it.

APPLY YOUR SKILLS 12.3

Publish a Report in Word and Format It for the Web

The main portion of the Active Listings report contains data that needs to be included in a report Homestead Properties personnel are preparing. In addition, they want to include data contained in the Sold Homestead Properties report on their website. In this exercise, you will publish one report in Word and then save the other as an HTML document for use on the web.

Before You Begin: Your as-Homestead Properties 2003 database should be open.

1. Open the **Active Listings** report and export it to **Word** as an RTF file, **saving** the report using the default filename and storing it in the folder with your student files.

Because the report contains a subreport, Access will display a message advising you that the subreport data cannot be processed. Because you want only the main report data in Word, that's okay.

2. Respond to any error messages by selecting the option to **continue**.

3. Review the report in Word and **exit** Word.

4. Switch back to **Access** and close the export dialog box.

5. Export the **Sold Properties** report to an HTML file that opens after the export is complete and use the default filename.

6. **Accept** all default HTML options.

7. Use **links** at the bottom of the web document to navigate through the pages of the HTML file.

8. **Exit** the browser and then **close** the dialog box in Access.

Critical Thinking & Work-Readiness Skills

In the course of working through the following Microsoft Office-based Critical Thinking exercises, you will also be utilizing various work-readiness skills, some of which are listed next to each exercise. Go to labyrinthelab.com/workreadiness *to learn more about the work-readiness skills.*

12.1 Publish and Export Data

Personnel at Foxy's gym, the workout facility that iJams employees use, want to include examples of database objects on their website, but are hesitant to publish personal data. As a result, you need to add a fictitious record to the Personnel table and export the record to a separate HTML file to provide a sample for online review. Use the ct-Foxy's database (Lesson 12 folder) to publish a copy of the Foxy Personnel form that displays the fictitious record in Word. Name the new Word file **ct-FoxyPersonnel** and print a copy of the page of the report that displays the fictitious record. Then export the Sample Personnel form in HTML format for use on the web. Print a copy of the web display.

WORK-READINESS SKILLS APPLIED

- Serving clients/ customers
- Using computers to process information
- Understanding systems

12.2 Create a Hyperlink

iJams has agreed to add Foxy's logo to the iJams Sales Personnel form in the iJams MultiFormat database that you created in this lesson and hyperlink the logo to ct-Foxy's database. They believe that this will reduce the amount of confusion that sometimes results when new personnel join iJams and want to use the exercise facility. Add the ct-Foxy's Logo (Lesson 12 folder) to the appropriate form in the iJams Multiformat database. Then, add a hyperlink to the iJams Sales Personnel form that opens the ct-Foxy's database (Lesson 12 folder). Position the hyperlink just below the logo. Finally, print a copy of the form. (Depending on the security settings active on your computer, you may be prompted by a security message to confirm that you want to continue. Click Yes to complete the hyperlink.)

WORK-READINESS SKILLS APPLIED

- Serving clients/ customers
- Improving or designing systems
- Seeing things in the mind's eye

12.3 Explore the Hyperlink Data Type

Hyperlinks added to forms and other database objects enable you to access database objects, files, and websites by clicking the link on the form or object. Access also contains a Hyperlink data type that formats text typed into the field as a hyperlink. Search the Help files to learn more about the Hyperlink data type. List in a Word document named **ct-Hyperlinks** saved to your Lesson 12 folder five fields that you might include in a database that could be formatted using the Hyperlink data type. Print the document. If working in a group, be prepared to discuss and defend your choices.

WORK-READINESS SKILLS APPLIED

- Improving or designing systems
- Acquiring and evaluation information
- Thinking creatively

Index

Notes

Notes

Notes

Notes

Notes